MW00397793

EXPAND

Leadership that Moves, Fulfills and Changes the World

Shannon Graham

Copyright © 2018, Shannon Graham

www.shannongraham.com

All rights reserved. No part of this publication may be reproduced, distributed, or transmitted in any form or by any means, including photocopying, recording, or other electronic or mechanical methods, without the prior written permission of the publisher, except in the case of brief quotations embodied in critical reviews and certain other non-commercial uses permitted by copyright law.

ISBN: 1986763080

ISBN-13: 978-1986763080

Table of Contents

Shannon Graham

The current model of leadership is broken.

Outdated and responsible for a wake of collateral damage.

I am seeing it to an end.

Though not by raising my voice or putting my fist in the air.

I'm creating a model that makes the existing system obsolete –

A model that allows every single person inspired by the movement of an individual or organization to become leaders.

A model that fosters multidimensional expansion.

Beyond the "three P" system of people, planet and profit, this new way includes a metric that has been left behind, until now.

Unprecedented change is on the horizon.

Introduction

The expectations of leadership have turned your dream into a nightmare. Fear and uncertainty rule far too many of your decisions, and a bottom-line focus is most often driving your behavior and identity. There little depth to your work, and the impact once defined by your vision has all but vanished. You are feeling the walls of the leadership box closing in, and the pressure is almost insurmountable. Striving for continuous achievement seems like the only favorable distraction from the need for deep impact that is overtaking you.

From an external perspective, you have an organization that works, though the internal culture falls far short of what it could be. There is a lack of trust and borderline resentment from the employees towards leadership, and the angst is reciprocal. You feel frustration that those within the organization are not showing up the way you know they can – the way you need them to. You've lost sight of who you are and where you are going, and everyone can feel it. Your growth, desires and happiness have become insignificant, washed aside in the overwhelming linear drive for achievement.

Despite being surrounded by people, you feel isolated,

frustrated, and disconnected from everything and everyone…with no idea of how to reignite your initial vision or change the current game. What you are feeling can only be described as hopelessness, and you don't know where to turn. It seems that so many other leaders are feeling just the same, and it's hard to read the survival instructions from inside the box. What you want is liberation – freedom from the pressures and expectations that are ruling you.

What started off as a dream has now become a prison sentence.

If you have created something that's helping the world in some way, shape, or form, should your ultimate reward for that be isolation, depression, and unhappiness? That seems very unfitting. If you've had success, but your family life sucks, your health is total shit or your organization is in turmoil, should that be how it is? No. That is a bastardized and downgraded version of not even what things could be, but what they *need* to be. It's not about starting over and creating something new; it's about bringing everything back home, because it got off to a bad start.

For too long, a limiting, one-dimensional model of leadership has taken us by force, creating a mindset that has been tolerated because of the global results it can produce. This bottom-line-driven model is the lowest minimum standard. The resultant fear-based culture creates competition where there should be collaboration, resentment where there should be respect, and contraction where there should be expansion. As long as someone is creating something that's changing the world, we've been willing to overlook some of the atrocities that exist. Classifying a leader as great simply because they can build an empire, even if they may not be excellent to their people along the way, doesn't cut it. In the name of realizing our personal, organizational and global potential, we need to change the standard by which we define and accept what leadership is.

In 1906, a time proceeding the triumph of the government-run, standardized public school system over private institutions, Dr. Maria Montessori opened a housing project in the district of San Lorenzo, a slum district of Rome, Italy. She, the first woman doctor in Italy, was driven by her desire to take care of young children based on a belief that "the 'secret of childhood' is that all are born with potentials and the adult should help that potential." In her vision, teachers would "help rather than judge," and the teacher should be there to "direct, guide and help children to learn with the attitude of love and acceptance." One year after she opened her doors to care for young children, "Casa dei Bambini" (Children's House) was opened. The classroom that set the foundation for what we see in Montessori schools today.[1]

Maria believed it was her duty to promote the rights and liberation of children. She saw children as "eager for knowledge

---

[1] http://www.dailymontessori.com/dr-maria-montessori/

7

and capable of initiating learning in a supportive, thoughtfully prepared learning environment."[2] In fostering the human spirit and the development of the whole child (physical, social, emotional, cognitive), she identified a need for the education system to shift to be more potential-focused, giving children the guided freedom to choose their work. Instead of the teacher being the focal point of the classroom (the source of learning), the class became child-centric and children supported each other in their learning and development.

When the public education system was created, children were being raised to work on farms, or in mines and mills. Times had changed, though the foundations of the education system remained the same.[3] Having children sit quietly and stare teachers leading from the front of the classroom was no longer conductive to helping children realize their potential and operate at that capacity as they grow up. Through her education methods, Maria Montessori created something that expanded upon a child's curiosity and creativity, rather than stifling them by putting the child in an institutionalized box with preconceived notions for what they should do or be. She helped children become limitless.

Today, there are 4500 Montessori school in the United

[2] https://amshq.org/Montessori-Education/Introduction-to-Montessori
[3] http://www.peacefulvalleymontessori.org/traditional-teaching-method-problems-montessori-schools-address/

States and 20,000 worldwide.[4] The success of schools is said to be due to a disenchantment with the urban school system, and parents wanting a "more humane, yet challenging" alternative to the long waiting lists. Recent research has also supported that the Montessori approach is in alignment with how children learn – by being given them freedom to be creative and to realize their potential.[5]

The need for a shift in the current leadership model is no different than the need Maria Montessori saw within the education system. You are a rebel, misfit, disruptor or and maverick. You are the Maria Montessoris or Steve Jobs of the world, who love to break the rules. Because of your creativity and innovation, you are really good at changing things, though not necessarily the right things. In the past, you've focused your efforts on innovative products or practices, when what really needs to shift is the model in which you are operating.

We're all pioneers, but we're doing it in a non-excellent model with non-excellent methodologies, as if Maria Montessori was trying to bring her programs into the existing public-school structure. Within the restrictive confines of the current leadership model, you are like the children or teachers in the public-school classrooms: not able to realize your exponential potential. You are

---

[4] http://www.montessori-namta.org/FAQ/Montessori-Education/How-many-Montessori-schools-are-there

[5] https://amshq.org/Montessori-Education/History-of-Montessori-Education

trying to extend the boundaries of the existing box, instead of choosing to operate *outside* of the box and become limitless.

When you're a rebel obsessed with breaking everything from rules to paradigms in the non-excellent vehicle of the mainstream model of leadership, you end up breaking others things, like your long-term happiness and fulfillment. You're breaking the morale of your company, your family and yourself. No matter how much you try and expand, the truth is that you will always be limited by the confines of the box in which you operate. Here's the great trap of leadership today: so many cookie-cutter leadership rules and pillars that you try to fit into ultimately stifle and kill your creativity, self-expression and growth. They suppress the deepest impact of your rebellion. Try as you might, you will not discover limitless happiness and fulfillment until you break free from the box.

Leadership began as a servant to us, though as it became institutionalized, it ended up as something we became a servant to. In the mainstream model, the singular focus is achievement – a zero-sum game realized without compassion for people or concern for positive global impact. Leadership is broken because it's one dimensional and non-inclusive of some of the most fundamental aspects of being a great leader. It has been built within a context of a results-orientated, commercially successful institution. Our world has changed, but the model has not.

The new era model of leadership needs to contain three critical pillars: the passion of impact, the art of fulfillment and the science of achievement. We need to regain the essence of what leadership is. No longer can you live in a bottom-line-driven-box and operate by unrealistic expectations and pressure for who and what a leader should be. It's time to deinstitutionalize and revolutionize leadership, to have it once again become our servant.

Leadership is not intended to be a restrictive box that imprisons you; it is intended to be a framework for expansion. *EXPAND: Leadership that Moves, Fulfills and Changes the World* is about burning the limited aspects of the old model to the ground and playing a totally different game, a quantum game. When you combine innovative and rebellious action with a sustainable and fulfilling approach, you get a limitless model that creates exponential growth.

This guide is for a very small group of people: the thoroughbreds who will have the highest probability of taking the transformation that I'm about to share with you and transmitting it into universe-denting power. It is for those who are willing to muster the courage to operate outside the box and beyond the typical restrictive definitions of leadership.

Why go through the angst and frustration of trying out a new model of leadership? Why go through the challenge of changing to a new era? Why not stick with the one-dimensional, results-focused model when it is works and is all too easy to default back to? Because you don't want to. You aren't okay operating inside a non-excellent model. You want something more, something better...and what you want matters. For the highest probability of deep impact, the vehicle must be excellent. You've been trying to fly to the moon in a VW bug. Now it's time to build yourself a star ship.

The New Era of the Expanded Leader

The topic of leadership has been covered for years, and yet, there is one missing component; one aspect that is drastically overlooked and undervalued. Many leadership books focus on organization-wide actions, mission statements, trust-building activities and the like...and while this is all important and valid, it leaves out the most important piece of the puzzle: the founder or the leader themselves. Though it may, on the surface, look and feel like it, this is not just another leadership book. This is about a revolution of self, and of your identity as a leader. It's about not being willing to sacrifice the founders anymore.

A big myth perpetuated in the success world, is that massive financial success equals happiness and contentment. However, there is a difference between *the art of fulfillment* and *the science of achievement*. What I have observed in many people who have been highly successful in business, is that achievement is favored over fulfillment, because fulfillment is a non-linear, multidimensional path. It requires emotions – feelings that you probably don't want to feel. It also requires you to reconcile parts of yourself that you may not want to look at. There is also no clear-cut path for it. It's not science or mathematics, and it takes courage and creativity.

This isn't to say that the bottom line isn't important. It sure is…but it's not the most important. There's something to diversification and focusing on the things that really matter. The more dimensions you are willing to look at in yourself, the better; and the more depth you are willing to create in each one of those areas, the better. Ultimately, what this expanded model enables is being a more complete version of yourself, so you can bring more of yourself to your work. After all, if you as a leader do not feel whole and complete internally, how is it possible to bring the best version of your vision to life?

In the broadest sense of the word "success," you can have it all – commercial success while nurturing your relationships, maintaining health, and finding fulfilment and happiness along the way. This multidimensional perspective is what's really important in this new era, because so much in our world is changing. Technology is constantly changing, the way that education is going is changing, the financial world is changing, travel is changing…everything is changing. We need to create new definitions and new metrics that mirror this multidimensional change.

The journey captured in this book is a departure from mediocrity, or what best-selling author and business consultant, Jim Collins describes as the transformation from "good to great." Up to this point, you've likely settled – for who you are, where you are and what you have. Reading this book is about making a decision to raise your standards and to raise your ceiling for what you believe is possible. When you do, your vision expands, and the ceiling become the floor.

This process is going to require great courage, not unlike the greatest breakthroughs in human history. You are making a massive shift away from limited, tyrannical, results-driven leadership, because you choose not to live by that model. You already have an inkling that there's a way to achieve the expanded model of leadership that is distinct from what you've done in the past – a method that will allow you to fully connect with the principles and identities of what it means to stretch your goals, realize your vision and be radically self-expressed.

This new definition of leadership is centered around irresponsibility – being bold enough to be yourself. Under the old model, responsibility often equates to modeling a perfect "illusion" of leadership, which leads to you sharing an untrue version of yourself. It ultimately means you're not radically self-expressed or radically developed, because you believe have sacrificed all the wrong things. The irresponsible, expanded leader is someone who shows up with more confidence, clarity and connection, not only to themselves, but to the people in the organization. There is a feeling of being whole; and on the outside, the organization is more powerful overall because the employees are cohesive and synergistic. Leaders create leaders.

Leadership has to be about developing ourselves, because an organization can only expand in direct relation to the expansion of the founder. The paradigm has to shift, because what you want matters and how you live matters. Leadership is passion and a state of being, and taking the leap outside the box of mainstream leadership will help you realize these two pillars of the new era. Welcome to a means to leadership that is powerful and limitless, rather than frustrating and defeating.

The fundamental difference of the new era is the leader who is transcended in a way – who is a part of something bigger – also feels whole and complete in who they are and in how they can move their vision forward. This piece is the key to unlocking transformation in an entirely new era, not only of leadership, but of changing the world in a way where the echo effect transcends all our lifetimes. Without having to exert energy or feel the stress of the chaos of the old model, extra bandwidth is gained to be innovative, creative and to continue pioneering. The leader becomes a visionary – someone whose inner-game discipline is reflected in there outer-game results.

The tyrannical leaders in the past have been followed because of their vision – it was good, powerful…and we all have an innate desire to be a part of something bigger than ourselves. In the expanded leader model, the prior ugliness of the old model gets transformed, so that employees feel free to fall in love with the vision – wanting to be connected to, inspired by and driven by it. They want to follow the leader, not because of an "if you don't you're gone" kind of thing. They do because they feel connected to not only the vision, but the leader – someone they aspire to be around or to be like.

Happiness and success within the company is a function of the leader's own happiness and success – from a fulfillment perspective, not a financial one. All of the metrics of the organization and of the end-user experience are and must be reflections of the founder themselves. Personal leadership is taking responsibility for all these external things – compassionate teams and deep impact for both the investor and end user. Think about the global synergy that gets created within this model. You have synergy that comes from a global shift from competition to collaboration, and awesomeness that comes from individuals having amazing experiences in their own lives. From the depth of these two elements comes the creation of a culture that leads to even more richness, innovation and creativity.

We are moving into an era of whole and complete leaders, where the reward for individuals being highly successful is not to become stressed out and miserable. As revolutionary as it sounds, the reward for creating world-changing companies and cultures can be contentment, happiness and fulfillment. This book is a declaration to say, "I don't care whether you're leading a movement or an organization or yourself through space and time – it is all about realizing the best of you and continuously evolving."

The graveyard is the richest place in the world because all the hopes and dreams and the songs of people's heart go there to die, because for the most part, they don't get expressed. You owe it to yourself to do what's in your heart, to realize the personal satisfaction and joy that comes from that. The world at-large has benefited the most by people who have followed what's in their heart.

Knowledge does not equal power; it is the application and transformation that comes as a function of integrating knowledge that makes one powerful. This book is designed to be a field guide. Think of it as a training manual because the contents here in or not to be taken lightly. Let them speak to those desires in your heart. At the end of every chapter, you will be encouraged to stop and to not only think, but to implement and take action.

What you get from this book is entirely up to you. It is time to take responsibility for getting exactly what you want in reading this book, in your role as a leader and in your life. You either have a gift or you ARE a gift, and the success of your company depends on your success. Shore up all parts of you that are the best and shore up the parts of you that are the worst, so that you can be a whole, complete leader. In this very moment, you have the opportunity to live in full expression of yourself and the full realization of your potential – to experience the totality of what it is to be a expanded leader.

Let us begin.

REDEFINING

LEADERSHIP

MYTH:

Massive financial success = happiness

TRUTH:

Leadership must focus on fulfillment and happiness as the richest parts of life.

The Mainstream Model

What is the cost of your current reality?

There is a big myth perpetuating the success world, that massive financial success equals happiness and fulfillment.

This is not the case.

Constantly chasing achievement, you are suffering inside.

The flip side of the myth is a picture of two worlds: the art of fulfillment and the science of achievement.

Two worlds that are connected, but not directly related.

You can simultaneously have fulfillment and success,

Though there's a catch.

The instructions on how to get to the new framework are one the outside of the box.

Trapped inside, you may feel as though you can't read them.

Pain and pressure bubble over, forcing you to an alternative.

In the current results-driven model of leadership, we've

had leaders who are very good at driving things forward from a business perspective, but they've faced significant personal challenges. Their family-life is suffering, or maybe they're not so great to the people in their organization because the results are driving everything. Selling a company for 250 million dollars is classified as admirable, and something to strive for...if that's what you want. Does happiness follow massive success? Most often no. Bank accounts are full, yet these people are unhappy and unfulfilled.

Dispelling the myth that financial success equates happiness is not to say that money can't help you be happy; it simply reflects a very separate, distinct path to creating fulfillment and happiness. This path is multidimensional, reflective of who we have become and what our ever-changing world has become. Leadership must include happiness and fulfillment, because those are the richest parts of life. They are the parts that we can dive into without suffering and sacrifice, allowing us to really be nourished and enriched by the experiences of life. They are the parts that are missing in the one-dimensional, mainstream model of leadership that places financial success above all else, including the founder.

Markus "Notch" Persson, a video game programmer, released an alpha version of his first big game in 2009. Five years later, "Notch" sold that game – known to us as Minecraft – to Microsoft for $2.5 billion. He declared that he made the sale for his sanity. Having grown up without much money, he thought that should he ever become rich, he would become someone who never spent his money. Following his massive financial success, he bought the most expensive house in Beverly Hills for $70million.[6] With media reports of extravagant parties abound, his interview and Twitter feed told a different story: one of a man who was lonely, lost and unhappy. His feeds became controversial, showing the pleas of a saddened billionaire – a case that didn't sell with those who knew suffering of a different nature.

The reality of the achievement-driven mainstream model is that successful people like "Notch" are suffering, but they can't talk about it, because it doesn't seem right or just. It doesn't seem like someone with that level of success should complain about anything…yet the pain is very real.

Imagine selling your company for a quarter of a billion dollars, and you wake up in the next morning and the many mornings thereafter feeling a lack of purpose, bored and uncertain about what to do next. In record time, the buzz of the money dwindled. You've bought all the toys, had all the experiences, and yet, there's this gaping hole that you don't know how to fill. It feels like despair. It feels like depression. It feels like massive isolation, because you don't want to engage with other people if you don't even have the capacity to engage with yourself. The reality would be not unlike Markus "Notch" Persson's tweets that described a

[6] http://www.dailymail.co.uk/news/article-3220333/The-whining-billionaire-says-rich-sheer-hell-Inside-life-Minecraft-founder-Markus-Persson-says-ruined-money.html

lonely man who spent his days starring at his face in the computer monitor.[7]

If you're lost in this world of figuring out how to be fulfilled and happy as a successful founder, but you can't navigate it, what can you to do when you can't confide in anyone? Often times, the answer is to continue to isolate. From the outside, everything looks like it's fine, which makes matters worse. As a convenient out, you start a new venture and race on to the next thing to avoid staying in the pain any longer than necessary. The easiest answer is often to jump back into another business, because it's what you know and what you're good at. This tactic only helps you avoid the real problem: having to answer the question of how you realize true fulfillment. In an interview with Forbes, "Notch" spoke of the future in terms of abandoning anything that looked like it could become successful.[8] His financial success had left him depleted of passion, happiness and fulfillment.

Where has your success left you?

Time and time again, we see stories like Notch's play out to different degrees. Those who have risen to financial success and

---

[7] http://www.dailymail.co.uk/news/article-3220333/The-whining-billionaire-says-rich-sheer-hell-Inside-life-Minecraft-founder-Markus-Persson-says-ruined-money.html

[8] https://www.forbes.com/sites/maxjedeurpalmgren/2015/05/06/how-markus-persson-built-a-video-game-into-a-phenomenon/#62fe53be2bae

have all the hallmarks that society says you need to be happy become some of the most disconnected, unfulfilled, unhappy people. As Tony Robbins would say, the ultimate failure is getting exactly what you want in life and not having it feel the way that you thought that it was going to feel: "success without fulfillment."[9]

According to the World Health Organization, more than 300 million people worldwide suffer from depression.[10] A 2015 University of California study states that a whopping 30% of entrepreneurs are likely to suffer from lifetime depression.[11] This begs the question: do the rewards for massive success include isolation, depression, and unfulfillment? Is this the way it needs to be? This statement is an important one because of the number of successful people who end up miserable, or worse.

There is an existing paradox in our culture that encourages massive financial success yet publishes an increasing number of stories about incredibly successful people who are unfulfilled and unhappy. Is it not strange that we, as a society, continue to be motivated to reach for an end destination that leads to isolation and

---

[9] https://www.inc.com/bill-carmody/tony-robbins-success-without-fulfillment-is-the-ultimate-failure.html

[10] http://www.who.int/mediacentre/factsheets/fs369/en/

[11] Freeman et al, "Are Entrepreneurs 'Touched with Fire'?" 2015 - http://www.michaelafreemanmd.com/Research_files/Are%20Entrepreneurs%20Touched%20with%20Fire%20(pre-pub%20n)%204-17-15.pdf

depression?

Is it not strange that we, as a society, continue to be motivated to reach for an end destination that leads to isolation and depression?

In the new era, this all-too-common reality must not and cannot be true. The must be a redefining of leadership that includes fulfillment for the founder from the onset. Happiness and fulfillment are not intended to be a prize at the end of a lengthy rainbow, after a big exit, or following a million or billion-dollar payday. Buying into such a story only turns your dream into a nightmare and leads you to arrive at a perceived end, only to discover that the intended fulfillment doesn't exist…which, in turn, leads to further chasing and greater despair.

Add to the current perception of fulfillment being an end-result a second trap that drives an unfilled leader deeper into despair. After realizing that the toys, experiences and money are not going to bring you fulfillment, you actually feel unworthy of happiness. Focusing on having a big impact on the world and striving for commercial success get used as creative avoidance. It's a potent combination – constantly striving while internally suffering. The resultant feeling is not only one of sadness, but also of hopelessness; and unlike the model that lead you to success, there's not a clear-cut path to escape these feelings.

Here's why the model of leadership needs to expand: financial success can be achieved by someone able to mathematically calculate their way to the top but finding your way through isolation and depression to happiness and fulfillment is a non-linear path. It's multidimensional and always changing – a reality that the mainstream model of leadership and someone with a linear or mathematical focus are not equipped to handle. Therein lies a formula for madness. You try everything that is supposedly needed to create these feelings of fulfillment and nothing happens. You are trapped in your nightmare with no idea how to break free from the box…and not only do you feel ill-equipped, but you have also become conditioned to not be fulfilled.

How long does it take to reach a high level of financial success? Let's say five to ten years. That's five to ten years you've conditioned yourself every day to not be fulfilled, to not be happy. This is what the linear, bottom-line-driven model of leadership has created in our world. Habits are very real, and they can hard-wire you. You've denied yourself for so long that your default state is unhappiness.

The Organizational Impact

Adding to the horror of the results-driven model of leadership are the expansive organization effects. The one-dimensional leader and their impact on the organization falls into two categories: the tyrant leader and the leader who doesn't know what they don't know. Both are limited, restricted by their own lack of knowledge. The effects on the people in the organization can be equally devastating. Many notable tyrant leaders have or are operating with borderline sociopathic tendencies, which some say are critical for success. They have non-excellent motives. As reported in the *Handbook of Psychopathy*, those with sociopathic or psychopathic tendencies "may achieve personal or professional successes at the expense of family, friends, and coworkers, leaving a swath of broken relationships in their wake."[12] They also lack empathy and have a disregard for social rules. Leaders who don't know what they don't know are arguably just as dangerous.

What if you could walk into your organization and know everyone was there because they wanted to be?

Imagine walking into an organization where you know most people are there for the paycheck, and they aren't passionate about or committed to your vision. This is a stark contrast to what is possible. What if you walked in and you knew everyone was there because they wanted to be there? The life of a tyrannical

---

[12] https://www.gwern.net/docs/psychology/2005-patrick-handbookpsychopathy.pdf#page=480

leader is rough, because they know their people either don't like them or don't want to be there; and as a result, they feel isolated and misunderstood.

In the 2008 Batman movie, *The Dark Night*, Harvey Dent says, "You either die a hero, or you live long enough to see yourself become the villain." Many so-called "tyrannical leaders" start off with the right intentions, but because they chose a linear, one-dimensional, achievement-focused path, they become hardened and jaded over time. People are not showing up or performing the way that they want them to, and they need to become the bad guy to achieve the objective success. They become the person they promised themselves they would never be.

I don't think anyone wakes up in the morning with an idea to start an amazing company and become the bad guy. It happens because you don't understand how to be fulfilled and feel whole. There may be a lack of understanding about the importance of hiring and culture. Driven by the bottom-line, everything becomes black and white, rather than being a living, breathing organism. Such a focus makes it easy to start off on and lead from the wrong foot: hiring the wrong people and neglecting to build a passionate culture. You don't understand that people, like passion, must be cultivated. You aren't motivated to create a compassionate and creative culture for yourself or the people you hire – even if you hire the "right" people. The eventual transition is one of descent in darkness, as you realize that in order to get what you want, you have to operate with an iron fist.

What ensues is a fear-based culture, where employees are running scared and not wanting to interact with the leader. What does it feel like from an employee standpoint? It feels like you're an asset, but not in a good way. Your value comes from your production and it's never enough. You're valuable until you're not – until you don't play by the rules or you don't live up to the expectations. There is a fear of being fired unless you do better, and you don't want to be yelled at or reprimanded. People don't feel safe, nor do they feel seen. Collaboration and synergy are non-existent, and employees are not given the freedom to expand. They continuously contract, keeping their heads down; because as long as they don't lose their job, they're okay. Not only is the impact visible between the leader and the employees, but also between the employees themselves. The environment becomes cutthroat, where people feel like they need to hide their motives of expansion, because they don't want to get beat to the punch by someone else. They fear being trampled on or backstabbed; and all of the effort that could be exerted to moving the organization forward is deterred, being used to watch one's own back.

As a leader of a fear-based culture, you're constantly on the lookout for where to put your thumb down. Who do you need to threaten to get what you want? All that you're achieving is an overuse of bandwidth. It's tiring and not how you really want to show up...even if it feels like how you need to show up to get what you want, if you even remember what it was that you wanted to create.

This tyrannical model is the lowest minimum standard. The fear-based culture creates competition where there should be collaboration. It creates resentment where there should be respect. And it creates scarcity and contraction, where there should be abundance and expansion.

Why is it then that tyrannical leadership remains at play when we have the potential to shift to a new model of leadership? Is it really that difficult to make the shift?

You want to be more compassionate to your people and develop a passionate culture, but based on what you've experienced, it feels impossible to connect this into reality and do so in a way that is whole or complete. We all know that change at the organizational level is difficult and takes time. If a leader has challenges with a new way or new leadership concepts, and things reach a tipping point where they become too much, then it is all too easy to default back to the tyrannical way. Why? Because it works. Not only does it work, but some of the biggest and most "successful" companies in the world use it, so it can't be that bad, right? Wrong. If you truly want to do things that matter you must include excellent standards of measurement along the way. The means cannot be justified by the end. This is the challenge of shifting the old paradigm: that the old model works...at least from the standpoint of financial success, though we need a new model that thrives on multidimensional expansion in every moment.

Why go through the difficulty of changing to a new model of leadership?

You want to change because you know that the path to success in leadership has become a slap in the face to human potentiality. We've been told that "to achieve success, there must be sacrifice," and that it's impossible to do it any other way. Up until now, when it comes to realizing our potential, you only want to know how far you can go or how high you can jump, before you have to cap it. This is where you suffer and experience pain, because you know there is more – more that you want to have and more that you have to give.

You can be fulfilled and commercially successful at the same time.

The current state of the mainstream model of leadership is that the organizational culture is in shambles, and the happiness and fulfillment of the founder are not part of the equation. The thing with impossibility is that it pre-assumes that you're not resourceful enough, dedicated enough, or powerful enough to figure out how to realize success without sacrifice. It shortchanges your potential, when it should not. There is a better way, a new way. You can be fulfilled and commercially successful at the same time. Welcome to leadership without sacrifice.

The Art of Fulfillment

It's time to sober up to the pain of what's going on in your life, and how much it's costing you to experience it. You're not going to change based on something you should do, but you will change based on something you must do. How much pain are you really in? What is it costing you mentally, emotionally, relationally and spiritually? Take out let that pain be your motivator. Take out feel that and act from there.

What is the current state of your life and business?

What is it costing you to stay in this reality?

Need is like inadequacy masquerading as ambition. Isn't that right? In this day and age of a performance-based culture, it's easy to mask need. It's easy to mask inadequacy, fear, doubt, shame, guilt and unworthiness with ambition. We live in a world where we tend to numb and distract ourselves from how we're doing, or how we're feeling, or how we're being. You can be having a terrible day and when someone asks "How are you doing?" you just say, "I'm great." Part of the problem in the mainstream model of leadership is that on paper or externally, everything looks good, and we want to champion that. The expanded leader vision that I want you to get on board with is a complete 180.

The new era of leadership is here, and that means leadership is going to look and feel very different than it has historically. This shift is going to change the landscape of what it means to work for an organization, and the perception of what leadership can be. Global change is making it critical for us to create this new model of leadership. We are stepping into a sea of constant fluctuation with a fairly high level of uncertainty about how to navigate it, which creates a recipe for wanting to run away. Success becomes a favorable distraction. In the mainstream model of success through sacrifice, the leader's happiness, fulfillment, and in a bigger context, their expansion, get left out because the focus is on achievement. Expansion and achievement are not synonymous. There are plenty of people who have achieved at high levels without personal expansion – growth in the form of true happiness and fulfillment. They have succeeded purely because it is a seemingly excellent form of creative avoidance. They creatively avoid feeling and becoming more, from the inside out.

Mathematical metrics don't require emotion. In the mainstream model, you can almost be more successful if you don't have emotion. It becomes easy to favor achievement over fulfillment in order to drive everything for the bottom-line. The new era leadership model shifts this paradigm. It is founded upon a non-linear approach to becoming an "expanded leader" – a person who embraces and cultivates the art of fulfillment and the science of achievement with the passion of impact. The vision is one of quantum synergy, where the leader is healthy, self-expressed, self-actualized and self-expanding.

Expanded Leadership focuses on:

Art of Fulfillment + Science of Achievement + Passion of Impact

At the foundation of expanded leadership is a leader who is self-expressed, self-actualized and self-expanding. The art of fulfillment and the science of achievement are two very different worlds. They are connected but not directly correlated. Science is very black and white, and it's formulaic and mathematical; art is unrestricted and colorful. The reason it's called "art" is because what fulfills one person is not the same as what fulfills another. Two people can look at the same piece of art, and one of them can be inspired and the other disgusted. The art of fulfillment is non-linear and multidimensional; it is messy and requires emotion and courage.

Has anything great ever come without real courage and risk? As a leader, you must have the courage to look at yourself and ask what is it that makes *you* fulfilled. In science, you can follow the hallmark metrics and rules of what companies in the past have done to be successful. As long as you stick with it, chances are that you'll hit the ball out of the park. However, if you follow someone else's metrics and rules of what makes them happy and fulfilled, it's almost guaranteed not to work for you simply *because it's not for you.* The art of fulfillment metrics must be customized. They need to be about not sacrificing yourself in the process of leadership, and about gaining greater self-knowledge. The process is about being willing to go to the depths of who you are to understand what makes you tick – what motivates you, fulfills you and makes you happy. You have to know what *you* want.

What does it look like when you are living in full expression of yourself?

What does that look like when your potential is realized?

What are the personal patterns

of excellence that lead you to be your greatest self?

How do you go about attaining those things?

There is a cost of operating below your potential and staying in your current cycle. These questions are one of the most personal endeavors a person can ever embark on – they are the pillars of this book.

A huge contributing factor to our suffering is when we stifle our expansion. It's different for everyone, but at some point, most people experience being put in a box. It's a combination of our culture placing you there *or* you putting yourself there. Either way, you end up inside a box that stifles your growth. Your knowledge and expression get suppressed. Furthermore, when something does not expand, there is typically not only restriction, but constriction. Slowly but surely, people who stay in a box too long suffocate. A life of quiet desperation is one where we believe the best – our greatest accomplishments – are behind us. I believe our greatest accomplishments are always ahead of us. To return to a state of expansion is to return to an explorative, inquisitive nature. It's returning to who we are at the highest level.

When you take an expanded leader and you have them lead

an organization, what kind of culture does that create? What type of impact does that create? When compared to someone who does the opposite, the need for the new model of leadership is clear.

The 4P Model

Release your vision from the jail or slavery it has been in.

You were never constrained by your vision,

It simply wasn't complete.

A critical piece was missing.

The vision didn't include you.

It's time for the principal to vote themselves in and be a part of the impact they so desperately desire to create.

How much more immersed, enamored, obsessed, and addicted you could be toward what you're creating in your life if you felt full?

Fulfill your desires and your potential.

Give from an overflowing cup, rather than an empty one.

Complete, whole, and safe, imagine the exponential levels of magic you'd create.

From healthy obsession and deep passion have come some of the greatest creations in the world.

It goes without saying that you have a big vision, and you want to create something that is going to have some kind of deep, positive impact on the world. Why then would you stay with a model that doesn't allow you to personally experience expansion and passion while having that impact – one that does not simultaneously allow for the art of fulfillment, the science of achievement and the passion of impact?

Historically, we have been stifled because of responsibility, and because we want to ensure an excellent bottom line of profitability. The consequence is that our expansion, our true self, gets left behind in the process because we sacrifice what we really want. Very often we do what other people want; we do what is needed of us. The challenge is that what other people want often isn't in our best interest…and what they want comes from a linear, one-dimensional place. It perpetuates a cycle where you, as a leader, leave yourself out of the equation. By leaving yourself out, the people who are connected to you follow suit…and that has become the model, the paradigm, for how things are done at large, until now. YOU are the added dimension to the new era leadership model.

The 3P Model = people + planet + profit

The 4P Model = people + planet + profit + principal

The expanded leadership model focuses on a 4th P – the principal – as part of a quadruple bottom line. At the forefront of the 4P model is the formative concept the founder (principal) creating a movement, company, product or service that is making a positive dent in the universe without sacrificing the good stuff along the way. The new era model includes a more complete picture of:

1. An understanding that massive commercial or achievement level success does not necessarily equal fulfillment.

2. A synergistic mindset that there doesn't have to be sacrifice, even if that's been the case historically.

In the mainstream model, too many leaders have become far too proficient at sacrifice. You've have been willing to let go of or not embrace things like your health or relationships, because you felt that the sacrifice was necessary in order to create commercial success. Maybe for you the reason sacrifice has become the default is because you do not feel worthy of having it all, or at least having the things you deeply desire most. There are elements of sacrifice that great leaders need to have. For instance, the captain has to go down with the ship. The new model reframes and redefines sacrifice by having it occur only in the right context – when it is not detrimental to the leader or your people. Sacrifice in the new model is about not waiting to feel how you want to feel, and not waiting for what you want to have. From this perspective, success becomes about not only business achievement or financial prosperity, but also about health, strong relationships, fulfillment and happiness along the way.

Not only do you not have to sacrifice, but by not sacrificing, it makes the end result even better because you are leading yourself first and showing others how to expand. Simultaneously, the legacy of a really great company becomes not what you have built or produced, but the hallmark of the culture you created.

Principal

The expanded leader is whole, complete, irresponsible, courageous and liberated. Irresponsible is being bold enough to be yourself and to be radically self-expressed. Under the old paradigm, being responsible means sacrifice. You're not radically self-expressed or radically developed. The mainstream model of leadership confines by not allowing for the expansion of the leader. Without fully expressing yourself, your vision, your impact and your organization can't fully express themselves.

The 4P Model flips the concept of sacrifice on its head, bringing in the overlooked, undervalued and fundamental aspect of the leader themselves.

In the new era, leadership has two pillars:

1. Leadership is Passion

2. Leadership is a State of Being

The first covers letting go of sacrifice and responsibility in order to have passion of impact. The second pillar is about living from the version of you that is whole and complete, and how you operate at your full potential in relation to people and planet. The expansion process metrics need to look at all aspects of the passion of impact, the art of fulfillment and the science of achievement. They need to focus on contribution, collaboration and impact in all four aspects of the organizational model: people, planet, profit and principal.

The new era motivators are contribution, collaboration and impact.

While the focus is on leadership of self, the reason for your work – the impact – must still have universal benefit. When you are doing big things in the world from a place of inadequacy or trying to fill a void, you make it about you. You are attempting to prove yourself to someone, and it's a selfish game. On paper, we've been willing to turn a blind eye because of the good that comes out of the venture. The right thing for the wrong reason is still the wrong thing. At the core of this new era of leadership, the motive is *we*, not me. Not because it sounds good to investors or consumers, but because YOU matter.

The *we* motivator comes from a desire to self-express without the need or attachment to acquiring fulfillment, significance or worthiness from an external source. You know these things come from within. This is important because it changes the motive. If you feel full and complete, then the mission not about you. It's not about what you need to prove or what you need to get; it's about what you can give, from a place of overflow.

If you look closely enough there are plenty of examples of leaders who have, whether by default or by some motivation that made them leap into this kind of leadership. They lived by the framework that leadership is a state of being and leadership is passion, and they change the world because of this.

To clarify, this is about *we* not *them*. Making your life all about other people at the exclusion of yourself isn't the way – that is the myth of required leadership sacrifice that we are busting. The martyr leader, who is all about self-sacrifice without fulfillment, is leading an incomplete process, giving without receiving. You can't give is from an empty basket, nor can you give from a place of internal lack. No matter how big the impact the leader is making, their individual life matters; individual fulfillment, abundance and happiness matter. Many leaders have sacrificed the wrong things not only that relate to themselves but to others in their organization. Often putting their own fear or greed before the people, the question that begs to be asked is why? Maybe because these leaders feel so abandoned internally so empty that fear and greed are their protection mechanism. From a place of being overflowing in the heart and soul a leader needs neither fear or greed.

Self-expression, at the highest level, is you being you.

Self-expression, at the highest level, is you being you. You've reincorporated yourself back into your vision. Leading from this place, the movements that you're making, and the dent you're creating in the universe, are pure art. We're going to explore all of the tools you need to create from this kind of depth and passion, because when you create a legacy where people can see that the leader is not someone who has to be all-sacrificing, it changes the paradigm. It allows other people to create something for themselves where they can become fulfilled as well. They too don't have to prove anything. They can act from a place of being whole, and that matters to collaboration and culture. From a big-picture perspective, this changes the ultimate end effect that you have on the world.

People

A large part of what the new era of leadership is creating is employees that become as transformed as the leader, through the process of simply existing in the organization. Their growth and expansion come from the impact that the leader is having on them. In addition, the workplace becomes an environment where the employee is free to take risks, be seen, and have the opportunity to grow.

In 2009, Amazon bought shoe retailer Zappos for $1.2 billon. Jeff Bezos did it because he wanted to understand Zappos' culture. Tony Hsieh, CEO of Zappos, stated the relationship between Zappos and Amazon was "governed by a document that formally recognizes the uniqueness of Zappos's culture and Amazon's duty to protect it."[13] Why did Bezos buy Zappos and allow them to operate independently, keeping their organizational practices and culture in tact? He may very well have done it because he wanted to study and understand the Zappos culture, and how it allows them to "deliver the Zappos experience to customers." In a video to employees, Bezos states that Amazon has always "obsessed over customers" (not competitors).[14] With a few years of studying would could be argued to be some of the best customer service of all time, Amazon began adopting Zappos' "Pay to Quit" model, which allows unhappy employees to leave

---

[13] http://fortune.com/2016/03/04/amazon-zappos-holacracy/
[14] https://techcrunch.com/2009/07/22/amazon-buys-zappos/

with payment up to one month's salary.[15] This, among many other practices, have visible effects with Amazon' and Zappos' people.

A focus on people leads to collaboration and an undeniable impact. Within Amazon, one employee serves customers by playing the role of Thor. In a recorded conversation uploaded to Imgur.com, the customer plays along without missing a beat. The interaction goes down as one of the greatest customer service moments of all time. When Tech Insider reached out to ask Amazon if they did in fact employee a "Thor," they replied, "We employ thousands of heroes like Thor in our customer service centers and we love when employees feel empowered to have fun and provide the best customer service possible."[16] A fear-based culture would never have allowed an employee to feel safe enough to take that creative freedom. When you create an environment where people feel safe and supported, it pours into benefits for the end-user. The employees expanded to the same degree as their leaders, Bezos and Hsieh.

Recently, I met a business owner at an event. He said, "I'm really excited to start this new venture, this new company, but I don't think any of my previous employees will join me…because I didn't treat them well. And that's sad to me." Wouldn't you want the total opposite? Wouldn't you want to be able to say, "We're

---

[15] https://hbr.org/2014/04/why-amazon-is-copying-zappos-and-paying-employees-to-quit

[16] http://www.businessinsider.com/amazon-customer-service-thor-2016-5

starting this whole new thing. Who wants to come?" and have everyone raise their hand?

You know the detrimental nature of the old linear model – of having a machine where employees are a cog in a wheel. What kind of culture, impact and personal experience is created when people clock in, clock out and do the same old thing every day, without expansion or growth? An expanded leadership culture is one where the employees feel valued, celebrated and encouraged to grow. There's synergy. The organization feels like being part of a family, and the leaders feel like they're part of a team, where they know they can rely on their people…and they don't need to lead with an iron fist. People show up because they want to, not out of the fear of ramification.

When a leader embodies the principle of focusing on transformation over transactions, the organizational impact includes creating a culture of expansion.

When a leader embodies the principle of focusing on transformation over transactions, the organizational impact includes creating a culture of expansion, where the employees are valued for their uniqueness and genius, rather than solely for their output. Employees are encouraged and given the freedom to expand. Many of Google's most valuable assets – Google News, Gmail, AdSense – came from the 20 percent time that they gave their employees to do whatever they think will benefit Google.[17]

As a leader, you're not only expanding an organization, you're expanding what is possible for people by giving them a model, an example. They can look at the organization and think, "Wow, not only is expansion possible for the bottom line, but this is possible for the culture within the organization." That is what's possible when you, as the leader, do not leave yourself out.

There is a large level of self-trust and love required to a take massive responsibility by allowing your people to have their own freedom to take responsibility. If we do not feel like we are enough, we project that onto others which makes them feel like they are not enough...and we feel like we must control them, because we pre-assume that they're going to get things wrong. This scenario has the leader living in the state of fear and reactiveness, and the employees live in the state of fear, trying to minimize the risk taking out of fear of being axed. In the expanded model, a leader leads from overflow and trust along with responsibility. When they the leader can trust themselves fully it allows them to trust others as well. Complaining rarely leads to solutions and worrying about the bad things that someone might do robs them of the potential. Your employees' excellence and responsibility are purely a mirror of your own, so if you are not

---

[17] http://www.businessinsider.com/google-20-percent-time-policy-2015-4

satisfied with what you are currently seeing then you by default, are the solution.

When you are whole and complete, you treat your people with compassion, because you have compassion for yourself. You can grow and pioneer, while having excellent health and relationships. To put yourself in the mainstream model box, where you have to sacrifice all these other things is outdated and limiting. It's also a slap in the face to our natural state of expansion.

If you are designed to expand in multiple dimensions, then why would you think you can only expand in one way, at the expense of other dimensions? When a tree extends roots down into the ground and grows up to the sky, it grows in multiple directions. They grow in multiple dimensions with ease because that's what they're designed to do. People are designed exactly the same, but we get trapped in a mindset that this isn't how it works. The new era of leadership is about changing the rules. This is not a new idea – it's a return to how you are and who you are. It's a return to the real truth.

The more attention you put on yourself and the organization, the more attention, capacity and bandwidth you have to put on the end user. The organization itself becomes a beacon for what's possible in the world regardless of the impact of their product or service. Zappos is a perfect example. Most people don't even know what Zappos sells; they know it's culture. The culture has inspired numerous other companies to live up to a standard of excellence as far as customer service goes. The company itself changed the world regardless of their product or service, because they chose to put customer service first.

Expanded leader,

expanded organization,

expanded world.

Planet

The more conscious you become about yourself as a leader, the more care and prioritize for yourself and for the organization, which creates a prioritization for the planet itself. Most typically, people who don't care much about themselves or other people also don't care about the planet.

Far too many organizations create a product or service that depletes the planet. The focus is on taking, rather than giving to the planet. We're taking without replenishing; nor are we giving the planet enough time to replenish itself. If we can't live in harmony with our planet, the inevitable result will be being forced to become so technologically advanced that we have to leave the planet and go live somewhere else. If we've totally screwed over our home, that's nothing to be proud of. Only a parasite kills its host and moves on.

The only reason to ever leave our planet should be that we want to. SpaceX CEO, Elon Musk, and Moon Express founder, Naveen Jane, have made it part of their missions to travel to Mars and the moon, respectively. We should only ever leave because we're curious and we want to explore...not because we've so badly screwed up our planet so badly that the irreversible damage no longer permits us to live here.

The 4P Model sets the foundation for care for people and the planet in a global basis, because the mindset is expansive. If you cut down one tree, you plant two – not just one, two. Planting one trees helps to save the planet, planting two helps to improve and expand it.

Profit

Years ago, I started using the language of legacy. Many caught on and followed. Legacy is far beyond a trend. It is not cool marketing jargon...though it is used that way. It is an echo of our soul's work – the timeless song to inspire generations to rise to their own masterpiece.

There are important pieces from the mainstream model of leadership that need to remain the same in the new 4P Model. These are the pieces that we have lost touch with, such as unshakeable care for the planet and building something generational. This means you create something unique that you are not looking to flip or exit from – something with longevity than supports planetary longevity. Being dedicated to quantum excellence from the onset means being open to whatever that necessitates of you. You invite that mindset into the environment of your organization, which is huge. You are founding a company you will stay in indefinitely, throughout your life, because it is your legacy.

In the new era 4P Model, profit stems from passion of impact – creating a legacy and focusing on the depth of your impact. It's about including all three pillars of the model: passion of impact, art of fulfillment and science of achievement. We all know that you can measure achievement; but you can measure impact as well. You measure the highest probability of deep impact by looking at the end user of whatever it is that you're creating and measuring their experience. That's the difference of the new model: the expanded leader doesn't measure transactions, they measure transformation. This applies to the end user the same as it does in relation to the people in the organization. The bottom-line becomes not "how many did we sell?" but "how deep did it go?"

The bottom-line becomes not
"how many did we sell?" but
"how deep did it go?"

How many people can you deeply touch? How can you build something that lasts many lifetimes? Achievement for achievement's sake, or profit's sake is not passion for impact. These days, everyone is so hyper-focused on scaling. You can't have a conversation with someone in the business world without scaling coming into it somehow. The challenge is that so much focus on scaling blinds people from creating actual impact. No amount of width necessarily equals depth. Scaling is important, but depth is far more important. If you're going to scale anything, scale the depth, the impact. If you can scale width and depth together, then great. The 4P Model focuses on depth first. If you only serve 1000 people, but you create a mile-deep impact with each of them, then you've done much more than an inch-deep impact on a million people. Numbers might look good on paper, but they aren't a legacy.

Doing the impossible and focusing on depth is so important because it's hard. It is difficult to figure out how to create really deep impact. It forces you to get creative and figure out how to do it. When Henry Ford told his engineers that he wanted a six-cylinder engine, they reacted by telling him that it wouldn't fit because they only had so much space in the cars. He told them to figure it out and gave them no other option. What happened? They figured it out. That is how you create expansion.

The leader that causes the people on the team all to expand beyond what's comfortable, normal or expected is the one who rallies them together to show up for the cause. If you really care, then prove it. Prove it by going deep, prove it by going beyond what you know how to do, and do something you don't know how to do. Give the end-user an experience that comes from something that you had to create rather than duplicate.

Give the end-user an experience that comes from something that you had to create rather than duplicate.

The objective is to create something that allows people to model it in the future, while simultaneously inspiring them to innovate. Create an organization that comes as a function of your wholeness, potential and full self-expression. Be a pioneer of what that looks like to be truly happy, passionate and complete in your success, so that future generations can have new models, new examples, of what it looks like to truly be fulfilled.

Could it be perceived as irresponsible to depart from safe, predictable patterns of the dry, cookie-cutter framework that has shaped leadership over the past few decades? Maybe. Though when your happiness and fulfillment, along with that of the organization and world is at stake, is the leap not worth it?

If you agree, let's go.

Making a Quantum Leap

Leadership is not an in-the-box experience.

Living inside the one-dimensional, bottom-line-focused model means restricting how much you're willing to give of yourself.

You're suffering because you're stifling your own growth.

There is no room for expansion.

Limitlessness and exponential growth only comes when you operate outside of the box.

Awakening is having a desire to break out.

You may not know how, but your desire is strong enough to push you to figure it out.

That's called resourcefulness.

Only outside can you become fully expressed and recognize your potential.

It's going to take a quantum leap to get there.

There's a glaring disconnect, a difference, between what you know and who you are. As long as you're not creating your life and business in the way that you want to, there will not be fulfillment – for yourself, the organization, the end users or the investors. This new era of expanded leadership about changing the game when being a leader isn't fulfilling that part of you that wants to feel fully alive. Nothing changes if nothing changes. You have to be willing to make the leap and break free from the limiting, one-dimensional model of achievement-driven leadership and go through the emotion-rich, multidimensional journey required to realize expansion, full self-expression and your full potential.

Rather than ask how you play this current leadership game differently, ask instead how you play a completely different game.

In order to change the game, you need to understand what you want, what those desires represent, and how you measure the quantum leap required to make your wants a reality. It's about seeing and moving into the future version of yourself – the one who is living in full expression and true to your full potential. Awakening to expanded leadership and this 4P Model integrates what you know into who you are and allows what you know to be part of your full self-expression. It means not being willing to live inside the box of the old model anymore.

While you've likely accumulated much knowledge through your experiences and studies of leadership, that knowledge alone isn't going to get you out of the old paradigm. You can know everything and still live in a box. The first step is making the shift to a new model of leadership is a big one: the leap. I want you to be prepared to go into some depths and face some of your shit, get uncomfortable and feel fucking irresponsible. You may even burn everything to the ground, yet you will still be willing to move forward because you're on board with realizing your best and being all that you are.

In your leadership struggles, you may have come to the conclusion that what you've built is completely unrelated to what you really want. Maybe you've built a software as a service company and if you're really brutally honest, you want to be an author, a full-time author. Or maybe you have a product business and you want to have a service business. You owe it to yourself and to the world to follow that thing that's in your heart, because that's what you need to do most as an individual. Walt Disney is a great example. He followed what was in his heart, despite people telling him that he had no original ideas. I don't know one person who hasn't been touched in some way by Disney, so thank God that he followed his heart and didn't downgrade his desire to do something else that was a mediocre version of what he really wanted.

What would happen to leadership if there were 100 Walt Disneys rather than just one? What would happen to organizations? To the end users?

Historically, real leaders have had to go outside of the box to create the most change. This is precisely why we need to create a new paradigm…though it is difficult to do so, because the ego gets attached to what we've built because we're proud of it. That pride and that ego is the exact same thing that keeps us closed from being whole and complete.

There is a fear that if you adapt a more "self-focused," irresponsible style of leadership, what you've build will fail. Will the production go down if you are obedient to your desires? Maybe, or maybe not. You could potentially lose, and you have to be prepared to essentially lose all that is, because two items can't occupy the same space at the same time. Something must potentially die or be dramatically transformed.

In the Indian culture, the God Shiva is the destroyer of worlds and galaxies – not only in a negative sense, but also in the positive sense of destroying the ego. In order to create something new and more beautiful, there has to be a willingness to destroy. The only constant is change. To be attached to something so much so that you're unwilling to look at anything else becomes detrimental and goes against the natural law of growth.

The natural law of growth is to expand and evolve, which

requires that you be real with who you are and where you are. Imagine reaching a level that is 10% of its maximum potential and capping it. This is partly why there's such chaos inside of you and inside of the organization in the first place. Our potential is not meant to be capped. It's a contradiction and oxymoron to have a visionary leader who has capped their vision because of things like fear, ego or old-model rules attached to what they created. Worse yet, they cap it because of the comfort and certainty that a restrictive model produces. There is safety inside the box.

In order to expand, you need to understand where you have been and what leadership has previously been known to be. You need to understand how old definitions and metrics have shaped your identity.

How did we reach this point of playing below our potential and full expression?

How Did We Reach this Point?

There is a very dangerous and detrimental paradigm occurring in the leadership world, which is that leadership is labelled in absolute terms as "X, Y, and Z." What that does is create unrealistic expectations and pressure for how and what many leaders should be. Leadership has become an institution; and within that institution came rules that don't make any sense for any leader to try and live up to. We get set up for failure because we feel like it is the responsibility of the leader to have it all put together…so if/when shit hits the fan, we have all the answers and can operate perfectly in a multitude of different areas. Who decided that a leader has to have it all figured out? When someone has a question and they come to you, you are expected to have an answer; if you don't have an answer, they feel like that is a direct indicator of your lack of knowledge, skill or ability. There is a side of you that wants to believe that as a leader, you have all the answers and do not make mistakes.

Who decided that a leader shouldn't have any flaws? With expectations for perfection in relation to employees, shareholders and the rest of the world, the leader contracts. The expansion process is created from this contracted space, which by default leads you to face your inadequacy and fears. The messiness of who you are comes out and unrealistic expectations get resolved. Some of the best leaders are those who have been willing to show their vulnerability in this process.

Part of being irresponsible and expanded means being vulnerable, willing to fail and open enough to not have the answers – to be okay with saying that you don't know. Being willing to ask for help when expanding is everything.

When it comes to your desires, are you willing to ask for help in realizing them?

The existing belief is that if you're not perfect or don't have all the answers, people won't respect you, and ultimately won't follow you. This is not true. The way you earn the respect is by being real. It happens by showing people all of you – being genuine, vulnerable, relatable and open – being willing to show people your humanness. Connection is ultimately the willingness to be seen in your totality. Without it, people who are following you and trying to live up to you, are ultimately trying to live up to an illusion...which only breeds conflict. So many leaders want to seem perfect or seem like they have it all figured out, so that's what they project onto their employees, so that their employees show up that way...when really, it's all a façade.

If you lead with perfection instead of raw passion and emotion, people will not feel you. Leadership is something others feel – it is passion and a state of being. People know when they feel it. How do you know that something is real? You feel it. How do you know that you're alive? You feel it. How do you know when you're in love? You feel it. How do you know when you are in pain? You feel it. How do you know when you're showing up powerfully in a leadership context? When other people feel it.

The challenge with the unrealistic expectations of leadership is that they obstruct and impede connection because you're so busy trying to manufacture that connection by seeming perfect and by seeming like you know it all. What you offer feels like something they cannot relate to…or, at very worst, feels fake. Too much perfection is unrelatable; too much all-knowingness begets disconnect.

Preconceived notions of what a leader "should be" are dangerous, because they make you believe that something beyond yourself is required or lacking. It essentially points at a level of unworthiness.

Because the organization can only expand in direct relation to the expansion of the founder, leadership has to be about developing ourselves. Even the best strategies become mediocre (at best) with a mediocre vehicle. Departing from mediocrity means no longer settling in relation to who you are, where you are and what you have. It means showing those who follow you the totality of who you are. Shore up all those parts of you that are the best and shore up the parts of you that are the worst, to become a whole, complete leader.

How Do You Change the Game?

It sounds counterintuitive to say that leadership is about self, though it is. It has to be. While most would say that leadership is about leading other people, the argument here is that if you can lead yourself, then other people will follow. Think about influence. How many people are attracted and love the idea of influence? Dale Carnegie's *How to Win Friends and Influence People* is one of the most famous books of all time…but who gets left out in that influence? Typically, the influencer. Why? Because they aren't great at influencing themselves. The same theory applies to leadership.

Personal leadership is the foundation of leadership – leading your mind, body and heart to the heights of your desire. It's about supporting the realization of your own potential. The Expanded Leadership Model is like "the Montessori of Leadership," because it's 100% about the individual. Just as Maria Montessori created an education system that was child-led – allowing children to foster the full potential of the human spirit and develop their whole selves (physical, social, emotional and cognitive) – it is up to you to create leadership that is leader-led, allowing yourself to be curious, expansive and child-like.

Maria created the "thoughtful environment" for children to initiate their own learning; this book is the framework to create your own expanded learning. It contains the tools to allow you to create an internal and external environment that fosters your potential and gives you the platform to ignite your passion. The real question is, once you insert yourself in that framework, where do you want to go?

This is leadership led from within, by you, as an individual. As a function of asking the questions you'll find here, and going through some of these frameworks, you come out the other side more whole, complete, clear and emboldened. The framework is built on questions because this is not a "one-size fits all" model – it accounts for your individuality. Instead of subscribing to someone else's secrets, you need to create your own personal patterns for excellence. I want to help you expand your passion and potential to their ultimate limitlessness, allowing you to have an identity that moves you forward, so that you can carry out your vision and find fulfillment.

No longer are you a servant to leadership; leadership returns to being your servant, your vehicle. The key of personal leadership ultimately comes down to a willingness to be courageous enough to be obedient to our desires. Growth is the most important journey you can embark on. Everything you want to be, do, have, and give is purely a function of your own growth and expansion…and you will never be more worthy or significant than you are right now.

You will never be more worthy or significant than you are right now

In his work of The Law of Sowing and Reaping, Jim Rohn says: "You don't reap what you sow, you reap much more." What this means is that if you have one pumpkin seed and you plant it and you get a pumpkin, though within that pumpkin there are upward of 100 more seeds. If you plant each one of those, there's 100 more pumpkins. You get the idea. Make your vehicle expansive and multidimensional.

In order to simultaneously realize success, happiness and fulfillment, you need to take the quantum leap – diving into the multiple dimensions of success – required to be a true revolutionary, be a more complete version of yourself and be true to your heart, fulfilling your desires. You need to plant multiple seeds and be open to and feel worthy of reaping their benefits. This means leading and influencing *yourself*. The goal is to have visionary leaders be commonplace, so that you would no longer have to idolize people like Walt Disney, Steve Jobs and Elon Musk…because they would no longer be rare.

How do you breach the limits of the old model and get to expanded leadership?

In order to play a new game, you need to work to improve your current reality and to bring your best future self into the present. By getting in touch with your desires and becoming fully expressed (living true to your desires), you move the needle forward. By getting really clear on who you are when you are living your full potential, you then reverse-engineer that version of yourself into the present. When the two dimensions intersect, you expedite the progression into becoming an Expanded Leader.

There are 3 steps to shifting the paradigm into expanded leadership:

1. Redefine leadership to incorporate 3 dimensions:

    -   The passion of impact

    -   The art of fulfillment

    -   The science of achievement

2. Take the quantum leap from where you are to who you know you can be. This involves using a multidimensional perspective required to live in full expression of yourself and realize your full potential.

3. Continue to expand by operating with a new set of motivators, renewed metrics and a totally different scale by which you measure success.

The metrics of the new era are a completely different unit of measurement. They are a quantum scale, measured by quantum leaps. Instead of going from 7 to 9, we're leaping from 7 to 70. It's about expanding to the point of your full potential and self-expression through exponential steps. There are no definitive

measures. The focus shifts from one of skill sets to one of fundamentally changing the global identity of the founder, and the trickle-down effect that has on the organization.

Diversification, through a focus on different dimensions of yourself and the organization, allows you to focus on what really matters. What happens if we diversified the so-called bottom line to be grouped by what's important, like a diversified metric portfolio covering happiness and fulfillment for you, your employees and the end user? Any successful stock investor will tell you that diversification is key to sustainability. It is no different for leadership success. The more dimensions you are willing to embrace and explore, and the deeper you go within each of them, the more you realize the all-encompassing effects of expanded success and its circular effects. The only set rule is continuous expansion.

Diving into the multiple dimensions of success allows you to become a more complete, expanded version of yourself.

The ultimate result of diving into the multiple dimensions of success is that a dedication to personal success and happiness allows you to become a more complete, expanded version of yourself; and that expanded version allows you to bring more of yourself to your work and the people in the organization. The organization cannot feel complete, move forward, and be successful and happy, unless the founder is successful and happy, period.

You can have commercial success while nurturing your relationships, maintaining health, and finding fulfilment and happiness. Quantum tactics, metrics and strategies allow for the realization of all of these because they are multidimensional. They are exponentially relevant and effective because they stem from a founder who operates in alignment with expansion. What does this mean? It means that in this new model of leadership, you are willing to take a quantum leap in order to simultaneously realize the passion of impact, the art of fulfillment and the science of achievement simultaneously. You are willing to do so even if it means destroying some of what you currently have or know, because you want to create compassionate teams, along with deep impact for the shareholders and end users.

Becoming an expanded leader happens when you are willing to embrace the multiple dimensions of yourself and of the steps needed to be the expanded leader. As a result, you:

1. Stretch your goals,
2. Attain your vision, and
3. Become radically self-expressed.

Leadership is not intended to be a restrictive box that stifles you and leaves you with no idea how to get out – it is intended to be a framework for expansion that you stand on to create your own rocket ship, to that you wherever you want to go. It's about limitless passion and self-expression. It's about taking the leap outside the box and into your full potential.

What makes this book and work distinct from the other leadership books that you have on the shelf is that we're not investigating a method for increased performance, we're talking about changing the game and redefining what leadership is. Leadership is intended to be passion and a state of being. Leadership has to start with you.

Phase 1 of the expansion process of the new multidimensional leadership model involves letting go of the idea of responsibility – sacrificing less and being more fully self-expressed. Phase 2 is about living from the version of you that is whole and complete – giving from a full cup.

Expanded leadership has two fundamental requirements:

1. To live in full expression of yourself.

2. To live in full realization of your potential.

The alternative to having no sense of how to make yourself happy, how to connect with others, or of what makes you fulfilled, is having an identity that is all-inclusive, expanded and powerful enough to grow a movement or a company past the moon without having to sacrifice the good stuff. It is quantum. The expanded leader says, "I believe I can grow a company past the moon by including these things. It's better for the world, the organization, and the bottom line to be fulfilled in my relationships, to care about my health, to experience organizational happiness, and to improve the planet."

What is currently holding you back from living in a state of full expression and expansion?

Ask yourself what is currently holding you back from living in a state of full expansion. If you are playing below your potential and without fully realizing your desires because you are afraid of failure or success, you've already lost. You have already robbed yourself, your family and the world of the gifts that you have to offer them. The scars that come with learning how to fly are significantly better than the perfect exterior that is dead inside.

If you desire to do something big and bold in the world, is that going to require more of you? Of course. You'll need to have more courage, more curiosity, more passion and more creativity. You're going to have to be a whole number of things, and you'll likely need to be a whole lot less of some things too. There will be a number of attributes that you must be more of, and some you must be less of – this is all part of your expansion.

The mindset of the new era is about not about sacrifice and exclusion at the cost of happiness and fulfillment; it's about understanding that through happiness and fulfillment you create the most complete impact possible. You create limitlessness. It's not about excluding things, it's understanding that *through* those things you get what you want.

At the core, whether you're starting something or your neck deep in something, making the quantum leap is about returning to the most important parts of the leadership equation and formatting an identity that is conducive to that. Identity comes with standards and expectations that you dedicate yourself to. It means expanding into your full expression and full potential. It's time to change the game, because you got off to a bad start. Passion and limitless potential are ingrained into who you are from the beginning, they are non-negotiable. That's why the greatest portion of this book is dedicated to redefining leadership to be about passion and a state of being.

Are you ready for a revolution in leadership?

LEADERSHIP IS PASSION

MYTH:

To achieve success, there must be sacrifice and responsibility.

TRUTH:

Being irresponsible is the most responsible thing you can do.

Phase 1 of becoming an Expanded Leader requires that you let go of the idea of responsibility.

The Art of Full Expression

You suffer because you are not insane.

The peak of this human experience is madness.

My whole life, I observed how people live mediocre, fair to middling, vanilla. Lives of quiet desperation.

I was not separate from them.

Within the cracks of the grey lies boundless color.

A place where words like "addicted" and "obsessed" are perfectly healthy descriptions of a life overflowing with passion.

When did safety overtake expansion?

It is far more asinine to live unfulfilled, unhappy and full of regret.

When you allow ourselves to go beyond the known and the comfort of the safety, diving into the depths of the moment and the experience, you feel saturated into the endless beauty that is life.

Give into the desires that call you forth, knowing full well that they desired you just as much.

The result is like gasoline on a fire.

Your life is a wonderful experiment to see how much you can be, do, have and give: untethered radical self-expression.

I believe that, to some degree, we are all a bit depressed. We are a bit sad and a bit regretful that we are not who we know we can be. Inside each of us is a yearning to live passionately, like artists with bleeding hearts. Leadership is no different than an artist seeking to individually express their creativity – both are forms of self-expression. They are both desire seeking expression. Similar to the artist who can never get enough, we suffer because we've restricted how much we're willing to give of ourselves, with regard to our own expansion. There is an undeniable, unescapable pain to knowing that you can be more, do more, have more and give more.

Expression is the opposite of depression. The ever-evolving definition of "the best of you" is the human journey played at the highest level. How much love can you give? How much love can you receive? How much can you grow? What can you really do? Who can you really be? What is the depth of that? What is the width of that? What is the greatest impact of that? It's a double-edged sword, because the journey comes with a lot of uncertainty and trials and tribulations.

Leadership is a reflection of your desire to expand into the unknown and into your limitless potential. We live in a culture where our desires are repressed and suppressed. This is as much about personal leadership, as it is leadership of an organization or a movement. When you are able to expand in all the dimensions you desire – and even some of the dimensions you don't want or intend to expand into – it's a valuable growth opportunity.

The difference between growth and expansion is that growth happens naturally. Expansion is a choice. When you're young you grow whether you like it or not, but you don't have to expand. A company that does well has all the puzzle pieces in place and grows naturally, but it doesn't mean they expand. To expand is to identify the dark pieces of who you are or assess the questionable pieces, and then venture into that darkness or unknown to figure those things out. Growth is linear and expansion is multidimensional and messy.

Having awareness of what you can make possible in your life and business is like setting gasoline on fire – igniting your wants into desires and giving you the strength to dig through the darkness to gain clarity on the journey with many unanswered questions. Being expanded means having a willingness to be all in. Feel the fear of the unknown, question what will happen, and then choose to leap anyway. We're conditioned to only risk and expand to the degree that we feel safe. Trust is what breathes safety to life – you have to trust yourself and the expansion process. From there, you leap, knowing that you will only realize what is possible for yourself when surrender and go all in.

What would be possible if you engaged with passion?

Since the dawn of man, fire has been a source of life, sustainability and growth. Passion is our fire, igniting possibility and potential in our lives. In the past, you have expanded because you had to in order to survive. In today's world, expansion is not mandatory – you can survive without it. The question is: is survival enough? Stagnation has led to suffering on a much deeper and broader level than growth and expansion ever could. Taking the leaping outside the current box in which you operate requires that you engage in passion.

What is passion? The Oxford Dictionaries define passion as a "strong and barely controllable emotion." It's not a thought or an idea, it's an emotion. It is a strong feeling of enthusiasm or excitement for something or about doing something – one that leads you to act in an irresponsible way. Passion is about having desire and heart. And if desire is expansion seeking to express itself, passion is the art of that full expression.

If desire is expansion seeking to express itself, passion is the art of that full expression.

Interestingly, the second definition for passion is "The suffering and death of Jesus." We have historically aligned passion with suffering. This is where the game changes in the new era of leadership: no longer does the founder have to be sacrificed. No longer do they get sacrificed for the sake of everyone and everything else. We're completely redefining the word passion. Jesus dying on the cross was not the end...he came back. Passion can be restored, renewed and redefined.

Passion is not intended to mean agonizing or being a martyr; it is also not intended to mean being tyrannical. One could argue that Pontius Pilate had passion when he sentenced Jesus to be crucified by the Romans. Passion must be directed for good: for our own expansion and that of others. If you look at how Jesus lived before his death, he was totally full. He didn't need anything, nor did he sacrifice his happiness. He lived with passion. The moment of his crucifixion, his suffering, did not fully define who he was or how he lived. He was able to give abundantly to others as he himself was overflowing.

You choose the standard by which you will live your life. We all know that we're going to suffer one way or the other – in the new model or the old one, inside the box or outside. You're going to feel pain one way or the other. What if you can choose to feel that pain as a function of your growth and expansion (so-called "growing pains"), rather than as a function of living inside a box? Wouldn't you be willing to trade or transform all the pain that comes along with the journey – the depression, sadness, unfulfillment and discontent – into fulfillment and full creative expression any day of the week?

Who can you be?

What can you have?

How much can you give?

Why is getting in touch with your desires (what you want) so important? When you come to terms with your desires, you understand your need to expand. I firmly believe that desire is expansion seeking to express itself. Not only do you have a desire to do the impossible in business, but you also have other everyday desires, and what you want matters. It's time to change the game, freeing yourself from the box where you stifled your potential or your everyday desires. Multidimensional expansion is no longer optional.

Take a look at anything in the world and observe how it behaves. Expansion is the law of the universe. Trees naturally expand to the peak of their potential; fish grow to the peak of their potential. Growth is built into everything. It is a natural human desire to expand and grow – to test the limitless bounds of your potential. We see it from the earliest stages of childhood: it's called curiosity. Curiosity is expansion in its infancy. Children have an insatiable desire to be, do and have everything. They're endlessly curious. The difference in venturing into the impossible as a whole and complete leader can best be described as being child-like. You become fascinated with the world, and you are clear on your desires. Imagination and creativity rule, as does collaboration. You believe in expansion.

Expansion is the law of the universe.

Curiosity is expansion in its infancy.

Curiosity is at the forefront of all leadership, pioneering, innovation and expansion. These are all forms of growth. Curiosity is about asking yourself the questions that provoke expansion. How curious are you about what you can do? About who you can be? About what you can have? About how much you can give? How can it be possible for you to be whole, complete and fulfilled, and create an even better bottom line? Sit with that concept and challenge yourself.

Passion and curiosity are soul mates. There is passion within curiosity itself. Desires (fueled by passion) are a pathway for your growth and expansion to come out. The expanded leader embraces and cultivates the art of fulfillment and the science of achievement with the passion of impact. The realization of your potential requires stretching your goals and vision to create what you want. This means bridging the gap between what you current are, do and have and what you want to be, do and have. Passion of impact happens when you are radically self-expressed. It includes exploring:

- What does it mean to live in full expression?
- How do you measure passion?
- How do you measure your impact?

Passion of impact, or full expression, occurs when you are creating something generational and focusing on the depth of your impact. It begins with the willingness to question your current versus ideal level of passion and understand why you do what you do. Expanded leadership is about letting go of responsibility and sacrifice, allowing yourself to grow. It's about allowing yourself to be fueled by and to fulfill what you desire.

What is your current impact?

What is your ideal impact?

What is driving your passion?

Personally, I have been dazzled by the cushy ease of being a lifestyle entrepreneur who has realized financial success: house in the hills of Santa Barbara, the sports car and lots of comfort and freedom. I've made great money teaching others how to create this for themselves...but it all felt amiss. Sharing my knowledge and experience through coaching was not fundamentally aligned with what I wanted. What I wanted to do was play a totally different game. It didn't matter to me how good I was at the game I was playing, because it wasn't fulfilling or fun, and it wasn't creating the ultimate impact I wanted to have in the world. And so, I burnt what I had built to the ground and changed the game.

There was an element of disobedience in my life because I wasn't honoring what I truly wanted. The truth is the cushy lifestyle was a great form of creative avoidance to my deep purpose. It was all created on sub-excellent effort. The metrics of happiness were not a driving contributor to my bottom line. For a long time, there were a number of things that I was unwilling to give myself. Underneath it all, were an uttered cry for acceptance and happiness. It culminated in a point where I felt as though I had reached the pinnacle of the value I could add to my clients, while denying myself happiness and fulfillment. Testing the premise of expanded leadership, I decided to see if I could create more by giving to myself the acceptance and happiness that I sought.

Deciding on an internal solution, I immediately started making exercise a priority and rekindled a second passion for video games. After growing up playing and loving video games, I reached a certain point in my business where I believed that "serious," successful entrepreneurs didn't have time for games. It felt that in order to be successful, I had to neglect that love. There's a habit in the world of success to neglect the things that actually make us happy and whole.

As years had passed without indulging in video games, I became more successful, on paper...and slowly but surely, I became more unfulfilled. Because as simple or distracting as they can be, video games are a lot of fun for me. It took giving myself the happiness I desired to give myself permission to play video games once again. Interestingly enough, my business hit record levels. Within the twelve months following my return to playing games, things accelerated to all-time highs...and I felt truly fulfilled.

When I emerged from the time of introspection, the conclusion was that I didn't want to get paid for my knowledge and my experience anymore, because that had nothing to do with my genius. What I had shared may have seemed genius, because others found value in the fact that the knowledge helped them drastically diminish their learning curve to get from point A to Z...but the truth is that it wasn't genius, because it had nothing to doing with what I actually wanted, and it wasn't me showing up at my full potential. Genius is being fully expressed, full expanded and living true to your full potential.

There were only a few metrics I could point to for creating that level of success I was realizing…and most of them were tied to giving myself permission to do the things that make me happy. As an expanded leader, I voted myself in, putting myself in the game of business like never before.

In the new business, my clients no longer hired me because of my knowledge or experience, or a desire to model my success; instead, they came to me for creative support for their desire to do things that have never been done. I attracted more people who were in a league all their own. The realm of the impossible beckons them. They know stepping into this unknown means challenges beyond anything they are prepared for. It also means they are willing to embark into a level of growth and leadership that is their true potential. They come to me to go on the expansion journey with them, because they understand that the echo effect of their legacy will transcend many lifetimes.

When I made the shift to sharing my imagination and creativity to help people answer questions for which the answers didn't yet exist, live out their passion and shape their legacy, I felt more whole, more capable, clearer, and more willing to risk and continue to rise. I felt happy and able to expand to meet the needs of those who were walking into the realm of the impossible. There was a fuel within me like never before.

Some people would call this state one of being highly

creative, impassioned, compassionate or curious. In the context of expanded leadership, it is called being fully self-expressed. It involves being deeply honest with yourself and others – a feeling of limitlessness. The expanded mindset is one of knowing that you can be, do, have, and give whatever you want. It's good for you and good for the world when you do what you want…when you do what makes you happy.

What makes you happy?

Most of us don't truly know what makes us happy. When asked what you want or desire, what most of us tell others is what you don't want. It happens because you have more knowledge of what you don't want than what you do want. Learning about what makes you happy takes time; it takes self-awareness. Expanded leadership has to do with you giving yourself the time and space to explore the greatest landscape and time space continuum that you will ever have the privilege to explore: yourself. Your organization, and ultimately, the dent that your organization makes in the universe is purely a reflection of you as an individual. It is a reflection of your happiness, fulfillment and expansion.

If your desire is to make a world changing impact, then with this shifted paradigm of multidimensional leadership, you must be the absolute best version of yourself – fully expressed and living in full realization of your potential. The highest probability of deep impact can only occur when you have become a whole, complete and expanded leader. What is a key precursor to this revolution of self? Happiness. Your happiness matters, your health matters, and all of the things that you desire matter. Passion fuels happiness.

When you are wildly self-expressed, there are no rules, no restrictions, no comparisons. What other people have and think is of no relevance to what you want to create. From an outside perspective, what you're doing and who you are is perceived to be completely irresponsible. This is freedom pioneering at the highest level (or at deepest level, depending on how you think about it). The first phase of the expansion process is centered in letting go of responsibility, and at the heart of it all is passion.

Make Passion a Priority

The longer you put aside the feelings and things you desire (passion), the less probable you are of ever having them, because you create patterns and beliefs about not having them that get reinforced over time. When you finally have the time and money to pursue the things you want, you then don't have the habits needed to support such a pursuit. In fact, you have a habit that pushes them in an opposite direction.

What often happens with successful people is they reach an exit point, which is supposedly the time when they "get it all back." However, because they have five, ten or more years of a habit built up of not indulging and embracing that fulfilment side of life, they don't know how to create what they want. So many of them race towards the next business, which that ultimately becomes a creative avoidance of being able to delve into those things they want. The result? A never-ending cycle of unfulfilled desires.

How did we reach this point of being on a perpetual circle to never getting what we want? This is the result of the old model of leadership – one of sacrificing the leader in the name of commercial success. It must stop here. The paradigm shift begins with your willingness to make passion and priority.

As a leader, there are two primary commitments that allow you to become and stay whole, expanded and complete:

1. Honor what allows you to be happy and fulfilled – live with passion and in full expression of yourself.

2. Honor what allows you to expand – realize your full potential.

What are some practices of happiness? You may be happy engaging with your family, being in nature, when you're exercising, while traveling or when you are being creative. There is no set formula or practice, because the answer is yours to discover. Asking yourself what allows you to be happy and fulfilled begins with adopting a much more expanded version about what happiness and fulfillment really mean. This redefinition stretches beyond the old school Buddhist-type, spiritual mentality of just being happy for happiness' sake. While such an endeavor is something noble to work toward, your happiness should be available to you whenever you want, without cause or reason.

Like expansion, passion is designed to be non-linear and multidimensional. Because it is emotion-based, it is intended to be boundless. Passion is designed to increase what you want and to take you anywhere you desire.

What is the current level of passion in your life and work?

Is that passion multidimensional?

Is your current mindset limiting you? The old, one-dimensional leadership model pre-assumes that the only way that you can produce excellent results is by sacrificing. It negates synergy and all parts of you that are whole and excellent – the parts that need to be activated to lead to even better performance and excellence.

It's time to sober up to how big you really are – how big you can be, and how much passion you can be responsible for having. Without intentional focus, it's not going to grow itself. If limitless passion and potential are possible for you, how do you want to show up to that?

Passion is the necessary predecessor to the realization of your full potential; it is the igniter to the expansion process. If potential is your vehicle, passion is the fuel that powers it. Even with an excellent vehicle, the extent to which it can take will be limited without serious passion.

What is fueling your potential?

Excellent vs. Non-excellent Drivers

What is driving your desires?

Wholeness? Contribution? Impact?

A need to win, get revenge or seek validation?

Caring about what other people think can be a powerful driver in the pursuit of what you want.

The leader who feels complete is very different from the one who is in need.

You cannot give from an empty cup, but that is exactly what you are attempting to do.

If you are unwilling to give yourself real unconditional love, you cannot possibly provide it for someone else.

If you cannot find worthiness internally, you will not find it from anyone else.

Nor can you realize it from your achievements.

The fuel has to be internal.

Everything starts within.

You cannot give something that you don't have or cannot

give to yourself.

Without giving yourself the passion and deep impact you desire, whatever impact you create for others is but a shadow of what it could be.

Giving from a full cup: that is the madness of being fully you.

Inside each of us is a yearning to live passionately. Your job is not to question or doubt your worthiness through the old model, restrictive definitions of what a leader should be, but rather to push the boundaries and expand your worthiness to its fullest extent. You need to recapture your worth in its innate unconditional nature. You were built to be passionate and to expand. No child is meant to finally visit Disney World to sit on the sidelines doubting whether they deserve to be there. Being in a leadership role means acknowledging that you deserve to be there and deserve to fulfill the limitless extent of your desires.

Why Do You Do What You Do?

You need passion to have impact, and that passion is powered by the drivers through which you choose to operate. In the current leadership model, the achievement-focused drivers that most leaders choose only lead to unhappiness. Creating a new leadership model, not only requires that we redefine passion, but also replace the drivers. This means replacing sacrifice with fulfillment and non-excellent drivers with excellent ones.

Motivation is why you do what you do, and motivation matters greatly. There are three types of motivation: you can play the game out of the fear of losing, you can play it out of the desire to win, or you play for the love of the game. In the old tyrannical model of leadership, people are playing the game out of the fear of losing. They don't want to lose, so they perform. There is a lot of stress and anxiety that ensue with fear-based drivers, and there is very little passion. When your bandwidth goes into fantasizing about the negative what-ifs, it cannot be dedicated to creativity and innovation. You are not allowing the best parts of you to be part of your reality. Playing to win is also a one-dimensional model. You have to win and there is a significant consequence if you don't win. There is pressure to perform.

The ultimate, expanded-minded motivation is to play the game out of a desire to play the game. The desire to win is good, but it doesn't necessarily mean that you love it. Loving the game isn't about winning or losing; it's purely about passion. There is no need to know or control the outcome. Many famous artists didn't have a desire to change the world with their art; they only had a desire to express themselves. They loved playing the game. Jimi Hendrix didn't care if people liked his music; he just wanted to play the guitar. He ended up changing the world.

Are you playing for the love of the game?

People who have achieved great things achieved them because of excellent motives – because they played for the love of the game. There have also been many of the world's most commercially "successful" companies that have had leaders that were driven by what we could argue are non-excellent motivations. If you're a driven, "type A," high-performance person, the desire to create and build something can also be a desire for validation of who and what you are, and how valuable you are, because you want to be significant. You want to be validated by having other people say, "I see what you're doing, and it's awesome."

Validation can quickly become a vicious cycle, as you attempt to prove the gifts you bring to the organization, and to the world. Enough is never enough. There is always a marker – be it making one million dollars, or a trillion – where you believe you'll get enough accolades, kudos and applause for your gifts to be satisfied or fulfilled. There is a sense that will be enough – proof that you have done something valuable and that you *are* valuable. Upon reaching the marker, you don't feel any kind of true fulfillment...so you determine that the marker must be ever higher. You then pour even more time and effort into a larger, more far-reaching marker, and the cycle perpetuates.

Without the capacity to feel loved and validated internally, it become easy to use global-scale success as a way to get love and validation. In this case, the desire to create impact and profit in the world comes from non-excellent motivation. They come from a place of need. Add in the fact that the majority of leaders also buy into a sacrificial lamb mentality and believe it's okay to sacrifice themselves in order to grow something that's either really profitable or makes a difference in the world. While striving for accolades, they leave out their health, relationships, happiness and fulfillment. At some point the cycle becomes so destructive that they've make an agreement with themselves to sacrifice their health and relationships and fix them later.

Andre Agassi never wanted to play tennis. In his 2010 autobiography, *Open*, he admitted that he had hated tennis. He played to prove to his father that he could. "Tennis interfered with my relationship with my father, and it interfered with the relationship with myself," he said in an interview with Oprah.com.[18] All that time, all those years – the blood, sweat, and tears that went into him being arguably one of the greatest tennis players of all time – and he didn't even love it. Achievement doesn't always mean passion. That time dedicated to proving something was time that Agassi missed out on what he really wanted – true connection to himself and to his father.

---

[18] http://www.oprah.com/spirit/andre-agassi-talks-about-his-book-open/all

When your motives are non-excellent, you'll do whatever is necessary to do what you set out to do.

When you look at your current motivators, are they excellent or non-excellent?

When your motives are non-excellent, you'll sacrifice your health and relationships (with yourself and with others) and do whatever is necessary to do what you set out to do. The reason for this behavior is that you don't believe you're worthy of what you really want. When you care what people think about you, you do not have a strong relationship of trust with yourself. Your value and who you are is derived from other people's opinions.

How Unworthiness Affects the Motive

Part two of the equation is how unworthiness affects the motive. Unworthiness is a powerful driver in keeping us deterred from what we really want. "I'm not enough" or "They said I couldn't do it" are non-excellent motivators. When it comes to our reason or motivation for achievement, many people are trying to fill a void, because they haven't mastered the art of fulfilment. They haven't discovered their unconditional inner worth.

A lack of inner worth plays out in many forms. Greed is a familiar function of internal deficit. When a person feels unprotected and unprovided for at the most foundational human levels, their greed increases to try and compensate. When a person is in overflow, their greed dissipates and their ability to serve the world becomes exponential because they are taken care of. They are able to focus on the bigger vision without distraction.

If you close your eyes and think about how worthy you are, what does that feel like? Allow yourself to feel how you want to feel, to give yourself permission to return to feeling as worthy as you want to feel. Now let me ask you, how worthy are you? How significant are you without your achievements? Don't list what you've accomplished or how much money you have. Don't list any performance-based results. What we're getting to is purely your essence. How does it feel to be you?

For many, there is a void in our lives that boils down to an objective with two contradicting motives: you want to dent the universe because you have a genuine desire there to do so *and* because of a feeling of not being enough. In the bottom-line driven model of leadership, you feel that you must thrive, succeed and create something in order to get recognition and be significant. Because of a sense of unworthiness, you are driven to play to win (or not lose), while ignoring the calling of what you really want. You end up striving for achievement and approval without heeding the call for love and connection that you need to give, achieve and have impact from a full cup. You are hoping that achievement will automatically create connection and fulfillment, which is in total disregard for the natural flow of human needs.

Abraham Maslow's Hierarchy of Needs points to love and belonging as the third human need (following physiological and safety needs). It is intended to precede the need success and esteem, though we've got them backwards. Wholeness – giving from a full cup – means you don't need to get anything and that you don't need to prove anything. The expanded model is about living and creating from a place of wholeness and fullness by cultivating passion and living true to our full potential. Passion must be the foundation of all that you do, because your achievement and potential can only become limitless when they aren't coming from a place of needing to prove that you are enough.

What is the source of your passion – it is from a place of need or one of already being complete?

What is passion ultimately about? It's about connection – a deeper connection to ourselves and to others. It requires continuous effort to live from a place of full expression – indulging in what makes us happy and giving to others from a place of wholeness and worth. It's about accepting the multidimensional exploration of fulfilling basic human needs within ourselves that we've lost sight of in our linear drive for achievement. You're trapped inside the leadership box, but you're not looking inside yourself for answers.

It's asinine to live unfulfilled, unhappy and full of regret; though the opposite isn't living with negative motives, revenge or an attempt to prove something. It's equally foolish to pre-assume that you can't produce amazing results in congruence with positivity, contentment and fulfilment. If anything, you would produce even better results when your identity is based on these elements, because they promote expansion for everyone involved.

Redefine your hunger to come from a place of fulfillment rather than need.

The new era shifts the paradigm of having the only way to get things done being from vengeful hunger (winning the game or fear of losing or needing to prove your worth). The hunger remains, though it's different...it's redefined. Revenge and sacrifice are one in the same: if you are out to prove something, you are sacrificing what you really want. The redefinition of passion to eliminate sacrifice means that you can still be highly motivated and also be truly fulfilled. You need to start from a place that is whole – without need for validation or revenge – rather than feeling incomplete and having something to prove. Passion comes from a full cup. Your motive becomes making a positive difference world and in your own life. As Frank Sinatra would say, doing it your way matters. Building what you want matters. Living with passion matters. Nothing to hide, nothing to prove, nothing to fear, nothing to lose.

Some people may argue that if you are happy, content and fulfilled from the beginning, and you don't have the fire, hunger, chip on their shoulder or some motive to drive you forward, then you won't have the passion to push forward. They believe that if you're really a visionary, there's going to be some major challenges along the way that you need that fuel to push through. My rebuttal to this is to look at some of the people who created some of the biggest dents in the universe that did it from love: Mother Teresa, Gandhi. They had fire for injustices that were happening, but by and large, their primary motivator was love…and they go down in history as some of the people who changed the world the most.

Just because some great artists or leaders have created from a place of depression or pain, doesn't mean you have to create from these dark places. Given the choice, why wouldn't you choose to create from a place of love and passion? You have a choice that is the point, you can decide.

If you feel incomplete, insignificant or unworthy, the need to prove yourself is one that has to be reconciled with a feeling of worthiness. Using revenge as motive does not reconcile the need. Motives and drivers can produce results, regardless of their intention. That's the double-edged sword of the matter: non-excellent motives can produce very excellent achievement-level results. The tyrannical model of leadership can lead to financial success. It's undeniable that it works, though is this the acceptable standard you want to have moving forward?

Getting the status, approval or validation will not make you feel complete, whole and significant. Feeling whole cannot happen externally; it must happen internally. External solutions are not the answer to an internal problem. Much like the false perception that expansion happens when you acquire something to make you more worthy, massive achievement is not the solution to unworthiness. If you want significance, you must live from significance, not for it. If you want worthiness, then you must live from worthiness, not for it.

If you want worthiness, then you must live *from* worthiness, not for it.

There is a level of borderline manipulation that occurs when you care too much about what people think, or want too desperately to prove something, because you're willing to do whatever is necessary to get others to think highly of you. Shifting the paradigm means being "resolved" – having a strong relationship with yourself and trusting/accepting yourself. It's okay to care what people think, but you have to remain unaffected by the people who don't agree or don't like what you're doing. To say you don't care what someone thinks is inaccurate. We all care, but a resolved leader doesn't require approval of others for their value. You care without being affected when someone doesn't understand or agree with what you're doing. You remain committed to following your passion.

To make the shift into expanded leadership, there is an awakening that has to happen to understand your worth and allow excellent motivators to drive your actions. More than understanding this conceptually, you have to live it. The awakening is the difference between knowing and being. In this information age, we know a lot of things, but very few of us *do* what we know. Over 70% of Americans are overweight or obese,[19] but if you asked those people if they know what to do to lose weight, most would say that they have some idea of what they could do…though they aren't doing it. It's not a matter of knowing, it's a matter of doing. The challenge is that your identity hasn't shifted. Your actions are a reflection of your inner identity. If your inner identity doesn't change, then neither do your actions.

The late, great musician Prince said, "Cool is being able to

---

[19] https://www.niddk.nih.gov/health-information/health-statistics/overweight-obesity

hang with yourself." We live in a day and age where it's difficult to do so…though it has always been difficult to hang with our self, to learn about our self and experience emotions that we may or may not understand, or thoughts that may or may not like. What do we do instead? We distract ourselves, and we now have more distractions than ever to enable this process. It's an art and science to create time and space for being with yourself. It has nothing to do with intentionality; it has to do with *being* in the moment with yourself, and allowing whatever thoughts and feelings come up. Become your own best friend. The longest relationship that any of us will ever be in is the relationship with ourselves, but that's the relationship most people sacrifice or neglect the most.

Understand that you have a choice in how you want to play the game and what you want to create. Choose to act from a place of being full and already feeling significant, powerful, and worthy. If you haven't felt that way until now, it doesn't matter because you can choose to change that starting today. You can make a big impact on history from a place of fulfillment and awesomeness. It's time to create what you want by cultivating your passion, while preserving your heart.

Cultivate Passion, Preserve the Heart

Love is a radical and unyielding emotion. Anger too.

Too often we only allowed ourselves to only lightly be touched by each and any of these.

Just enough to remind ourselves that they are real, that they exist.

Never enough to truly know them.

Consumed, immersed, engulfed – that is how these emotions are meant to be experienced.

Cultivate passion like children with no sense of boundaries who are free to race with abandon into their wildest dreams.

They don't think to put themselves down or care what others may think.

They are liberated to be reckless and fail.

When you finally decided that you've invested enough time in playing it safe, you ask for a better return on investment.

It is no longer enough to imagine what is possible.

You need to cultivate it.

To know something is to feel it. Love, inspiration.

A life lived alive, overflowing.

The thing that inspires people the most is passion. We love art because it's an encapsulation of someone's passion. That's why we love movies. That's why we love life, really. The passion of life is how we get the most out of this journey. When we're experiencing passion, we are the most alive. Being fully alive makes it easy for a leader to create a culture and a following, because everyone wants to be a part of something that is connected to passion. Their vision is filled with passion. Everyone wants to ignite the passion that is within, even if it means being connected to a bigger vision that's not necessarily our own.

Client Story

"It's not 'either or,' it's both." That's the theory by which Daniel Batten runs Exponential Founders – a globally unique program that grows the complete, unique skill-set that tech founders need to succeed. The first CEO in New Zealand to close an angel investment round, Daniel has played key roles in three separate teams that launched three separate $15-$120M valuation-companies worldwide. His current goal is to help grow five new $100M companies and five new $1Billion companies by 2021.

When asked about what it is to create a high-tech company, he says it's like having a high-performance motorcycle: it has huge power, but it's an absolutely death-machine if you don't know how to run it. "Everyone is focused on how to optimize the already-fast machine. If you teach the rider how to ride the machine, so there's not a 9-out-of-10 chance of spinning out of control, you have a much deeper impact."

How was it possible to build an expanded business without an expanded leader at the center of it? When he asked himself what he truly wanted, it was to enhance not just the business, but to help enhance the person.

Daniel was constantly seeing founders sacrificing their personal lives in the name of success. Trying to be a leader in business often felt like beating down a door. The approach that most people use is either to get so brutal with a full-frontal assault that eventually it caves in – you bang your ahead against it until either the door falls down or you do. The second approach is to diminish yourself to be so small that you can actually creep under the door. At every turn, the leaders around him were diminishing themselves to a fraction of who they are – sacrificing all dimensions of their beings on account that they might become successful. They would get through the door, but at what cost?

If you've spent years becoming a diminished version of yourself and never honoring what you want, then you've become really good at being the diminished version of yourself. You can't undo effects on your health, well-being, mindset, expansion, happiness and fulfillment. If you've realized success along the way, all you've done is become a rich, diminished version of yourself.

Success at the cost of everything else leads to suffering. You cannot work on yourself or your organization's culture later. As Daniel says, "Later is a twin sister of never. We as humans do not have a good track record of doing things that are obvious. We know that a plate full of vegetables is better for us, yet we choose a plate of burgers instead. We follow tradition at our peril. What we need are advocates for common sense."

And so, he became an advocate for common sense, extending beyond his capacity to launch successful startups. With a mission to increase the world's GDP (starting with New Zealand's) by raising the capability of a handful of entrepreneurs who can change the world, he set out to personally help more people who *can* change the world become people who *do*.

When Daniel came to Santa Barbara to work with me, I asked him what felt like the impossible task the he could help achieve that would massively dent the universe, his response was immediate and powerful: "I want to raise the GDP of New Zealand by raising the GDC." GDC is a concept he created that stands for Gross Domestic Confidence. In New Zealand there is a mindset

called "Tall poppy syndrome" which is a false sense of humility –
a limiting belief that causes people to see themselves as not enough
or less than others, robbing them of their ability to shine brightly in
the world. It was clear to Daniel that by shifting this national
epidemic, it would not only drastically increase the GDP, but also
create a strong and more confident people as a whole. He wanted
to help others reach far beyond not sacrificing, in order to
confidently expand to their fullest potential.

After a few days of combining our creativity and
imagination, we realized that Daniel needed to give people an
example of the impossible being possible. He found a
transportation inventor with a ground-breaking, rapid public
transportation system, who for ten years, due to a lack of
confidence, had kept himself from bringing his genius creation
forth to the world. After some intensive work, Daniel helped the
inventor change his mindset and belief system for what was
possible…and what happened next was incredible.

India got word of the invention and flew the founder to
pitch his idea to the Prime Minister of Transportation. Having
discovered confidence and clarity of how he could make the
impossible possible, the inventor sold his technology as a
revolutionary new mode of transportation for India. He became an
example to other innovators that they too could do something that
was never done before. He helped instill passion and confidence in
others…and he has subsequently helped raise New Zealand's

GDP.

Here's what's ironic. We have leaders who want to do the impossible, like going to Mars – things that have never been done before – yet what seems more impossible is having a balanced life. That's ridiculous. Expanding yourself is like finding the key to the door and confidently walking in, without diminishment or brute force.

Daniel puts a fundamental priority on caring about himself and the people he works with, so he doesn't let them get away with simply growing a business. He illustrates to those he works with that by growing themselves, while understanding and appreciating who they are and what they desire, they can turn that around and allow it to grow the people on their team and the business. In parallel, he has expanded his clients to think of themselves as leaders – thinking of their roles as bigger than they previously thought. They feel there are a part of a movement, where technology has become New Zealand's top export. These leaders are making business success possible with their own success at the epicenter.

He also helps his clients realize that the greatest impact they will make and the greatest legacy will leave is probably not through their technology or the customers they help – it's through the ripple effects of how they show up as a leader and on their team. He focuses on preserving the human heart – making a global impact in terms of the lives of the people they touch. Over the course of 10 years, Daniel has worked closely with 826 sales professionals, 147 sales leaders and 89 business owners and 31 CEOs of high-growth exporting companies. As proof of what is possible when you cultivate passion and preserve the heart, the founders in his program have a 100% success rate on raising both 1st and 2nd round of capital, overcome growing pains, become strong leaders, grow revenues exponentially, all the while getting home for dinner on time each night. It's not an "either or" scenario, it's both.

The idea, the concept, of having it all, indulging and being obedient to your desires is really wild. Side effects may include feeling free...not in the sense of being dangerous, but rather about feeling raw. They also include feeling unrefined, playful, fun and adventurous. In the context of the expanded leader, it feels irresponsible. Living a life of passion means being obedient to those moments of desire – the moments where you are brutally honest about what you want and make the choice to fulfill that desire. When Daniel answered the call of what he wanted, it felt expansive. When you answer the call, it will feel expansive. It is one of the most honest ways you can honor yourself. There is no sub-narrative telling us to be somewhere else or do something else.

Getting in Touch with Your Desires

With desire being expansion seeking to the expressed, one of the steps of the expansion process has to be getting in touch with your desires at a very clear level. This is the process of cultivating passion: listening to your desires without judgement or demonizing them. There is no over glorification of them either. Discovering your desires becomes much like a goal-setting process, with added vulnerability. Goal orientation is the impossible visualization process of creating a possible dream.

What do you want?

Why do you want it?

Why is it so important to you?

How passionate are you about what you currently are doing and about who you are?

Asking "Why?" is one of the most powerful discovery exercises you can undertake. It ultimately leads to your true motive, and the real vision of what you want to create. Get sobered up to how powerful your vision really is, to how much depth and dimension it has. Your wants are so much bigger than what you initially describe them to be. Ask yourself "Why?" to evokes the bigger version of yourself – to get a very clear picture of where you are and what it's costing you to stay there. It will show you where you want to be, and what that picture really looks like.

Is creating art as an artist not the cultivation of the passion? The more you do it, the more you cultivate it. The deeper you get into it, the more your heart bleeds. It's a cultivation.

How are you cultivating passion in your life?

Have you departed from what you truly desire to do what you felt was necessary?

How do you gain clarity when you have a feeling or knowing that you want something different, but don't know what it is? You do so by being radically honest with yourself, at the deepest level of who you are. First and foremost, you have to give yourself the time, space and permission to ask dig into the question of what you truly desire and be honest about the answer. There has to be a pause – a moment where a shift occurs and you say, "Okay, let me stop focusing on what I don't want." To cultivate passion, you have to stay with the problem.

Albert Einstein said, "It's not that I'm so smart, it's just that I stay with problems longer." If you give a question or problem enough time, you can get an answer, no matter who you are. If you listen and are willing to stay with the inquiry as to what you want, you will get the clarity you need to make a quantum leap. The shift the paradigm and redefinition of passion and leadership require it.

To cultivate passion, you have to stay with the question of what it is that you want.

When you ask yourself "What do I really want?" it can quickly become uncomfortable. The challenge with the question is most of us have been conditioned to not pay attention to what we really want. The question elicits a lot of what we've already covered: worthiness, doubt and many other emotional ups and downs. Leaders have been taught to want to sacrifice – to do for the good of everyone else. The required irresponsibility of the expanded leader begins with entertaining and engaging with your desires: asking for what you really want. While it feels like doing so means that you are taking your eyes off the ball and won't be able to produce at a high level, the opposite is true.

If you spend the required time, you can reach a point of clarity. Clarity is available to us all the time, but our judgments, doubt, worthiness and all other limiting beliefs get in the way.

When take the time to listen and make decisions from your heart (rather than your head), you find out what you really want and what really matters. From there, you make the choice to allow it to grow. Asking yourself what you want and why you want it is the starting point of the expansion process. When you are fully immersed in the experience and the richness that comes from surrendering to your desires, you are expanding. No longer are you stuck in old patterns, beliefs or methodologies.

Our cultural belief that desire will only lead us to places that are bad or dangerous is restrictive. That's inside-the-box thinking. While the belief can be substantiated by many examples of people who followed their desires to end up in train wrecks, there are a greater number of examples of those who were driven by desire only to create something that changed the world for the better. Elon Musk has the desire to retire on Mars[20] and has set a 2022 date to launch the first ship to the red planet.[21] All of his life, he has been a sci-fi and comic book geek…and what sci-fi geek doesn't want to go to Mars? Talk about being honest and indulging your desires!

I believe that those who got derailed from cultivating passion weren't really following their desires; they were most

---

[20] https://www.theguardian.com/technology/2010/aug/01/elon-musk-spacex-rocket-mars
[21] https://www.cnbc.com/2017/11/29/what-it-will-be-like-to-travel-to-mars-in-elon-musks-spaceship.html

likely downgrading their desires so much that they became toxic versions of what they really want. The most powerful example would be an addiction to alcohol or drugs – a false euphoria. Addiction to achievement can be equally as dangerous when it comes to creative avoidance that keeps us from indulging in our truest desires.

As a society, we're avoiding what we really want...and what we're all seeking is connection – preservation of the human heart. In a 30,000-mile journey studying addiction around the world, Swiss-British journalist and author Johann Hair identifies the opposite of addiction as human connection, not sobriety. His work points to years of research, as well as powerful personal anecdotes.[22] What happens is that when people become isolated, they seek out a distraction that will give them a certain feeling – a feeling good enough and strong enough to really depart them from how they feel, which is disconnected and isolated. They wanted connection and they either didn't know how to get it, or they were afraid to have the courage to get it.

Connection takes courage. It takes courage to tell yourself and others what you want, or to be open to hearing what others want. Cultivating passion takes courage. Thinking that our desires will lead to addiction or dangerous places is inaccurate. Self-destruction is not a bi-product of following our desires, and train

---

[22] https://www.huffingtonpost.com/johann-hari/the-real-cause-of-addicti_b_6506936.html

wrecks occur even when people don't follow their desires.

If this is true, then why do so many leaders lack passion?

So many leaders lack passion because they either didn't have it in the first place, or because they had it and tried to cram themselves into the box of what leadership has been taught to be. It is no different than a stifling education system. You take a kid who is full of passion and plug them into the school system and, very often, their passion gets lost. They lose their passion for learning because they are not doing it on their terms.

Many leaders start off with a passion, though being in a leadership position is a landscape that they're not used to. The foreign nature and existing definitions of what a leader should be are not a fit. There is a lot to learn, though rather than maintaining their passion and leading from it, they depart from what they truly desire and play it safe by doing what they feel is necessary or "responsible." They choose to learn the existing cookie-cutter, in-the-box methodologies of leadership, instead of cultivating their passion and creating their own methodology to preserve what's in their heart.

Passion is also easy to lose when operating in a linear, one-dimensional model of leadership. When the focus is on achievement and the bottom line, a leader can turn into a glorified manager who is telling people what to do. The passion for the bigger picture, the multiple-dimensions of the organization and of themselves disappears. The leader is left with a feeling that the people they are working with are not connected to the vision as much as they are, which triggers a subsequent decrease in passion. They are left feeling stuck and frustrated, spinning their wheels in a passionless organization.

The dilution of passion supports only one thing: the bottom line. That's exactly what creates a structure that is dry and one-dimensional, where you turn off your emotions and heart to focus on achievement and results. Empathy, compassion and the ability to connect are all stifled. If you're not a connected leader, an empathetic leader and a compassionate leader, then all you've got is tyrannical leadership. If leadership is passion, then the goal with any leadership methodology has to be to preserve the human heart (passion) at all costs. It has to be multidimensional and expansive. Your greatest achievements cannot be behind you. Leadership doesn't only require cultivating passion and preserving what's in the human heart, it depends on it.

The new era of leadership depends on the cultivation of passion and the preservation of the human heart.

How do you cultivate passion while preserving what's in your heart? Cultivating passion is about transitioning from doing to being. Leadership is passion and leadership is a state of being. The primary component to cultivate more passion is getting clear about what lights you up. Defining what are you passionate about can be easier than determining what you want. What has you feeling so strongly that you can't even contain it? What are those ideas? What are those conditions? What are those people? What are those visions? When you identify and pursue those things, you cultivate passion.

You only make time for the things that you absolutely must make time for. Make passion a priority. Cultivate it. Much like in relationships, if you don't make passion a priority, the relationship dies. Remember, passion is your fire. Cultivating it means putting logs on the fire continuously over time. It will not suffice to initially put on a big log and have it burn really bright. You have two choices: either the fire dies, or you put more wood on it.

How Do You Measure Passion and Impact?

In the new era of leadership, the most effective tool for measuring your passion and impact on people, planet and profit is simple: ask yourself how you feel. When you're on fire with passion, you feel a certain way. When you're not, you feel something other than. There are really only two worlds: one where you are on fire with passion, and anything other than that. Create a habit or ritual of constantly checking in and asking yourself, "How do I feel?"

Being on fire with passion means feeling full, in overflow, unstoppable, light and clear about what you want to be, do and have. The opposite end of the spectrum is heavy, unclear, not unstoppable (or stopped) and feels like burden, like a log doused with water. Create a visual of this spectrum and gauge where you are at any point by asking how you feel. If the scale runs from 1-10, where 1 is being stopped and 10 is being unstoppable, where are you? Where can you look forward to being as you continue to cultivate passion and progress through the spectrum?

This spectrum becomes your passion quotient (PQ) because it's a unit of measurement. You see where your current PQ is and how it can improve (where it can go). I believe that your IQ and emotional intelligence (EQ) can be improved, and your passion quotient is no different. Where do you fall? What do you need to do to move yourself forward on the spectrum?

How do you currently feel?

What does it look like externally, when your passion is fully expressed?

In the new era model, the 4Ps of principal, people, planet and profit are all driven by and measured in terms of passion – how you feel. Compared this to the old model, where the vision or mission statement may have some hallmarks of passion in it, but they are not ultimately founded upon passion. When you really drill it down, true, unbridled passion isn't there. In order for a mission statement or vision to have passion, the people in the organization need to have passion...and if the people have even more passion than the mission statement itself, then you're winning. After all, passion is about connection.

Leadership needs to always be human; and being fully human, fully alive, requires both the cultivation of passion and the preservation of the human heart. It requires that you and the things you do be messy, dangerous, emotion-filled and driven by desire. Passion is directly correlated to all of these things. It's about giving ourselves permission to be irresponsible and building the tools necessary to venture into the impossible.

Be Irresponsible

I'm obsessed with honesty lately.

Many of us have a habit of using words or phrases that water down what we *really* want.

What you're currently experiencing is either boring or fucking awesome.

That level of realness can feel like too much. It can be perceived as being too much.

When it comes to our full expression, it's time to push beyond the comfort of "pretty good" and get to outstanding.

The cost of not being responsible has become too much.

Is it responsible to diminish or completely nullify our own growth, desire and expansion in the name of a bigger vision?

We are modeling to future generations that everyone else comes first and our personal desires don't matter.

Perpetuating a cycle of glorified martyrism.

A belief is only as strong as your ability to defend it.

Putting yourself first feels greatly irresponsible.

That irresponsibility is the only way to create the type of impact you desire.

Draw a line in the sand for the ultimate picture of your legacy.

There is a side to leadership that has, for far too long, been perceived as "irresponsible." It is founded in a cultural belief that things like happiness, health and great relationships are *not* necessary inclusions in a leader's world. When these things are prioritized, it is classified as self-centered, given the "bigger" vision at hand. The pendulum has swung too far in favor of putting ourselves last. World health and happiness statistics support this sad truth. At this point in history, the majority of things that society would consider irresponsible are the things we need to focus on the most.

The biggest challenge of irresponsibility really comes down to feeling that putting yourself first is irresponsible. Shifting that mindset is the best thing you can do, because being fully self-expressed and having passion of impact requires that you be irresponsible. In fact, it's irresponsible not to be irresponsible, because being responsible very often means modeling to the people that your trying to be responsible for, leading with an untrue version of yourself and ignoring or nullifying your desires.

What ensues is having resentment for and being victimized by those you are responsible for. It leads the people in your organization to model the same behavior for themselves down the line. It's a lose-lose situation. Such "responsible" conduct presumes that you don't have the boldness, courage, resourcefulness or know-how to do things irresponsibly – that you can't pull it off or make it happen in alignment with your full self-expression and multidimensional potential. Such an assumption is very sad, given you are limitless. It is crazy to think that there are leaders who desire to do things never done before and are so bold and bright in the endeavor, yet they don't have the capacity to believe it is possible to create a life where they can have it all. They believe it is impossible to create a life where the foundational riches that life has to offer – like happiness and fulfillment – are not left out. Is this thinking not small minded and contradictory? Is it not a slap in the face to your full potential to believe that the ONLY way to achieve is to suffer the loss of critical pieces of oneself?

Of course, if "having it all" feels unrealistic and there are many examples to look at and see its impossibility. However, that does not change the fact that this mindset and model are limited. Don't you think it's time to give up being a mule for a shot at something more aligned with magic? Aren't we in the age of imagination? The magician in you is far superior to the mule. You don't have to remind anyone about the value of hard work, and we all know that life will sometimes be unbalanced. The bigger picture points to a radical departure from what is and what has been. Yes, this sounds irresponsible. How else would that which has never existed sound?

Before you jump to conclusions about what irresponsibility means, let's be clear about what it's not. This is not a book about the unpredictable or sometimes irrational leadership style that we see in modern leaders like Donald Trump, Vladimir Putin or Kim Jong-Un. This is about shifting the paradigm of a societal lack of self-care and self-love. Evidence for this necessary change is all around us. Mothers put their family members first to provide for them, and they suffer because their needs do not get met. Fathers experience the same. Founders put their happiness, health and relationships last in order to provide for the "greater good." On paper, such an approach seems noble and responsible, though when it comes to your overall fulfillment, it is actually a misdirected and detrimental focus. With the touting of everyday heroes, there seems to be such merit to a sacrificial approach…to the point that it has become the norm rather than the exception. Responsibility now encompasses areas of your life that should not require sacrifice in order to help others.

There is another side to responsibility where everything you create is your responsibility. We see many leaders who want to skirt or escape their responsibility; who look for the easy way out and they point fingers and complain when things don't go their way. The greatest leaders take 100% responsibility for *everything that is "theirs" to take responsibility for*. Suffering creates unnecessary pain. It's easy to become frustrated and suffer because someone isn't doing something correctly...though isn't it your responsibility to do so? In his book *Extreme Ownership*, Jocko Willink talks about the necessity for leaders to embrace extreme ownership. How many things are your responsibility? How many things have you been trying to take responsibility for that are not your responsibility? There is genius in knowing the difference.

There are two parts to the responsibility puzzle. The first is taking responsibility for absolutely everything that is under your control. As the leader of a movement or organization, in a way, this can mean everything. The second part, or the flip-side of this coin, is that many leaders refuse to relinquish control to people who can do specific tasks better than if they micromanage, helicopter over and ultimately stifle the progress of the movement or organization. The deepest possible impact is deterred because the leader is using bandwidth on micromanaging their people, when they should be using that power to take responsibility for something else – something that aligns with their full expression.

Put yourself under a microscope. Where do you put yourself last personally and professionally? Imagine for a moment what life would be like if you were to be in absolutely overflow in the areas where you have been in deficit. How much more joy and connection would you experience in your relationships? How much broader and deeper would your impact be if you were giving from a full cup and in a state overabundance?

Being irresponsible means giving to yourself in order to be able to give to others with the deepest impact.

In our world where self-care, self-love, self-nurture, self-parenting and personal development very often seem taboo when associated with leadership, we've gotten so far away from our own worthiness that it feels wrong to even think about yourself, let alone embrace self-care. Irresponsibility isn't a selfish pursuit. It means giving to yourself in order to become fully expressed and be able to give to others with the deepest impact. When you allow yourself to be irresponsible and expanded, it will reflect in how you treat your employees. The result is greater trust, communication, excellence, and overall richness in the organizational culture. The effects spill over to improve the experience of the end-user and their interaction with your product or service. It starts with you.

This book is not intended to appeal to the "everyday person," because the new era of leadership necessitates reaching for the impossible and being irresponsible. Both of these steps require operating outside the box and outside of your comfort zone. If you're on the edge, exhausted from entertaining theories of the old linear, one-dimensional leaderships model, you are ready. You can feel the need for the paradigm shift, because you realize how much playing on the responsible side of the fence has costs you.

Venture into the Impossible

Being irresponsible means being willing to venture into the impossible, knowing it is possible to have it all and do it all because you are limitless. Steve Jobs, Elon Musk, Henry Ford and Walt Disney could all see the impossible. They had visions of things that had never existed before, and they were willing to be irresponsible in order to create them.

What does being irresponsible require? It necessitates that you have the willingness:

1. To pursue something that had never been done before.

2. To go against conventional knowledge and counsel (the cultural voice that says, "It's not a good idea" or "It's a bad idea.")

3. To be the whole, full-expressed version of yourself.

When Elon Musk started Tesla, he faced scathing and ruthless attacks on his vision for electric cars. Did society really need them? Were we ready for them? Through the tough times of the 2008 economic crash, he persevered with his desire and vision, proving naysayers wrong. Over the course of the next decade, Tesla's success was so significant that it not only repaid the capital it sought out to keep the company afloat, but also paid interest to their investors.[23]

Being the whole version of yourself, true to what you want, is going to feel irresponsible – like you are going against convention. This is all part of the expansion process. Be a beacon for more than solely your "mission statement"; be an example that putting oneself first is the way of the future. Beyond whatever it is you and your company stand for, let that statement now include wholeness and expansion at both the individual and corporate level. The most responsible thing to do is to be irresponsible.

Be a beacon for more than solely your "mission statement"; be an example that putting oneself first is the way of the future.

Irresponsibility and venturing into the impossible doesn't guarantee success. However, many of our greatest breakthroughs are growth opportunities that have come from our mistakes. When you operate from a place where you aren't intentional about growing in certain areas of your life and business, and those areas

[23] https://www.youtube.com/watch?v=HxCH_lxQ4Nk

hit a tipping point (shit hits the fan), you then have to resolve them. This process becomes one of your greatest learning tools.

The dark side of the coin is that our identity often gets attached to negative aspects of failure. You think you're not enough or that you *are* a failure. Failure is an occurrence; it is not an identity trait. It is something that happens, it is not something that you are. When that failure is associated to as an identity trait, it knocks people off the horse and keeps them off the horse indefinitely.

An expanded leader sees failure as perfection, because an artist is never done creating renditions. They're never done creating masterpieces, even if many of their creations end up in the waste bin. Failure is part of the process, but they don't consider themselves a failure because of these experiences. They learn from it and move on, knowing that everything that happens is perfect, because it is part of the process.

If you knew you couldn't fail, what would you do?

What would you go after?

What would you try?

What would you create?

You'd likely try everything. There would be no limit to how much you are willing to attempt. That's what an expanded leader does. We're attached to this idea that failure has to mean something in order for it to not be a bad thing. The fact is that failure can just be failure. You don't have to finagle it and manipulate it into something. It can be just another attempt. Detaching from failure (not attaching failure to your identity) allows you to have a constant iteration cycle of progress, of forward movement. Instead of fearing failure, you can intentionally seek and find where your holes are:

What is it that you're afraid of?

What is it that you're avoiding?

Ask these questions and allow yourself to consciously, purposely go there. Spend the require time investigating what comes up. That's how you realize multidimensional expansion. The one-dimensional leader grows as a function of reaction; the multidimensional leader grows as a function of intention.

If we look at people who have had success on a major scale, we can see that they were willing to try more than most people. They were willing to fail more than most people. Thomas Edison arguably "failed" several thousand times to create the light bulb. From his perspective, Edison said, "I speak without exaggeration when I say that I have constructed three thousand different theories in connection with the electric light, each one of them reasonable and apparently to be true. Yet only in two cases did my experiments prove the truth of my theory."[24] He didn't count or identify with his failures.

There is a side to the human ego that's not willing to be wrong or to fail. Henry Ford was so ignorant, stating that he didn't care what he didn't know. He was dedicated to what he believed was possible…even when it seemed impossible to others. Had he asked his market what they wanted, they would likely have said "a faster horse." Sometimes the market doesn't know what they want; and most often, people do not know their potential. Ford was also willing to say that he had no idea how to progress and ask for help. When he began the creation of his famous V-8 engine, his engineers told him that it wasn't possible to cast the eight-cylinder gas engine block in one piece. He told them to "Produce it anyway."[25]

A lot of leaders feel it's irresponsible to ask for help, because they feel like as the "leader," they shouldn't have to ask for help. Ford had an attachment to what he wanted to create, but not to creating it alone or solely his way. His ignorance extended

---

[24] http://edison.rutgers.edu/newsletter9.html

[25] https://www.thehenryford.org/collections-and-research/digital-collections/artifact/126894/

http://dreamdolivelove.com/do-it/choosing-setting-goals/the-secret-of-henry-fords-success almost to the point of not having an ego. Was he even self-aware enough to know that he could do what he did? In a way, his actions were genius.

For the expanded leader, self-awareness is what matters – being self-aware enough to know what you want and being irresponsible enough to go into the impossible to get it. Irresponsibility ultimately ends up being true responsibility. It is really the only and best thing you can do. You need to open yourself up, to be open to the gaps or blind spots that you need filled and bring in those who can help us fill them.

Passion – having desire and heart – is one of the best ways that you can experience expansion in the realm of the impossible. Cultivate passion at all costs. Very often, your desires will bump up against things that you've never done before; that's why being willing to venture into the impossible is so important. When you desire to do the impossible, what that means is you have accepted one of the greatest growth opportunities that you can have. If you have a desire to do the impossible and you don't, you're stifling the very thing that can help you grow the most.

Venturing into the impossible creates growth opportunities at both a personal and global level. When you create for yourself, you most likely create something that impacts the world in a very positive way; and whoever comes along for the ride with you gets to grow by simultaneously experiencing the impossible with you.

What is the ultimate result of venturing into the impossible?

When you venture into the impossible, the "Bannister effect" happens. I believe that the "Roger Bannister effect" is real. In 1954, he broke the four-minute-mile. His record lasted only 46 days.[26] When he did it, other people believed that it was possible for them and they did it. Call it a funny coincidence, but it happened.

When someone embarks to do the impossible and indulge in their biggest desires, not only does it allow for personal expansion, it allows for global expansion by inspiring other people to indulge in their maximum desire. People in the world look at what you or someone else has done and say, "Wow, they decided to go after the impossible and they did it!" These people then start to think about the things they've been wanting to do that were previously considered impossible and realize that if you did what was thought to be impossible, then so can they. You create a ripple effect, much like "the hundredth monkey phenomenon."

While it is arguable whether the phenomenon is true or hypothetical, the story serves to make a good point about the effect of one person venturing into the impossible. In 1952, scientists

---

[26] https://www.britannica.com/biography/Roger-Bannister

were observing the Japanese monkey, Macaca fuscata, and leaving potatoes for them in the sand. While the monkeys enjoyed the raw sweet potatoes, they did not enjoy the sand. One day, an 18-month-old female monkey discovered she could resolve the problem by washing the potatoes in the nearby stream. She shared the new awareness with her mother and playmates, when then taught others. Over the course of the next six years, 99 more monkeys in on Koshima Island began washing their potatoes in the stream. The story has it that by the end of the day that the 99th monkey began washing their potatoes, every monkey on the island had begun washing their potatoes. The hundredth monkey was believed to have created the effect. Most fascinating to the scientists was that the breakthrough was not limited to the monkeys on that island – it was happening elsewhere too.[27]

This story alludes to the quantum conscious upgrade that happens when just one of us is willing to do what was previously believed to be impossible. Expansion is not limited to one vertical focus of doing the impossible (even if that is arguably the best focus); if there is to be totality and exponentiality in your growth, it must cover all facets of who you are. You must be willing and able to grow all facets of who you are. That way, whatever impossible vision you embark on will have an even deeper impact on the world.

Being irresponsible, venturing into the impossible,

---

[27] http://www.worldtrans.org/pos/monkey.html

cultivating passion and preserving the human heart are what allows you to have passion of impact and be fully expressed. Passion – the fulfillment of your desires – is the key components. Honoring what you want along the journey is what ignites fulfillment. These are the aspects of becoming expanded leader by letting go of the idea of responsibility and sacrifice.

If leadership is both passion and a state of being, the next phase has to be about living from the version of yourself that is whole and complete.

LEADERSHIP IS A STATE OF BEING

MYTH:

Your worth and self are defined by your achievements, role and performance.

TRUTH:

Even the best identity created in a linear, one-dimensional place cannot serve your multidimensional existence.

Phase 2 of becoming an Expanded Leader requires that you live from the version of yourself that is whole and complete.

Live Your Limitless Potential

What is your potential: creating a lifestyle or living a legacy?

This is about you and the world.

Many gifted leaders are fooled into thinking their highest existence is globe-trotting and having an automated business.

Truly gifted people are meant to play a part in the shift of the planet.

You must go through the major season of helping ourselves, because the shift to expanded leadership is needed.

The art of fulfillment is equally as important as the science of achievement, because you can only fully give when you are full.

Dig deep and create a totally different version of yourself – one that is whole and complete.

The work will be hard, though when the season is over, you will feel very different, expanded.

There will be a layer of ownership, commitment, and responsibility beyond what was previously known.

New feelings emerge that are beyond a rush of blood.

They are a heart on fire.

Departing from the known to the unknown can be intimidating.

You push on, because the point is not to have a business that gives you a lifestyle, but a calling that gives you life.

If one thing is certain, it is that your potential is far beyond whatever you believe it is.

What is the peak of human potential?

Not a single person knows the answer to this question. Why? Because no one has ever realized it. The best answer is that the extent of our potential is limitless. One thing is certain: we all have an innate knowing that we can be bigger than what we are. You might not know how big you can be, but you know that it's bigger, much bigger.

Why haven't we gotten there? Either you haven't had the time or the desire to go there; or you believe that it's just not possible to get there. The beauty in expanding into our potential is that once you reach a peak, you see that there's a new top to leap for. It was a top that couldn't be seen from the bottom, but once you get there, you realized there is more. What you've gained are a new perspective and a new vantage point…and you now have a completely different peak to strive for – one of exponentially more potential than you previously realized possible.

The one thing that we can all agree on is that there's more. Is it safe to say that there's significantly more to ourselves than what we've experienced so far? We are designed to expand; it's when we don't that we are out of alignment with the natural laws of the universe. Therefore, the best pursuit you can take is to continuously test the bounds of that limitlessness by immersing yourself in your passions and living from your full potential.

We've all had experiences in life where an emergency or opportunity occurred that we didn't have the time, knowledge, resources, or money for, but we made it happen. How is that possible? It's possible because our potential is far beyond what we typically demonstrate on a daily basis. Taking the quantum leap into living our potential is liberating, because we're not willing to be fooled into thinking that knowing is enough or that living inside the box of an old model is enough. You need to take the leap. Growing exponentially is not a concept you've never heard before. Now is the time to live it rather than know it.

The expanded leader is 180° from the picture of the one-dimensional leader who striving for massive financial success, achievement or employing creative avoidance of happiness by continuously sourcing success *because* they feel empty inside. The expanded leader lives from a version of themselves that is whole and complete.

The first phase of the expansion process is about letting of the idea of responsibility and sacrifice, while embracing the idea of being irresponsible...which is, in many ways, the epitome of being responsible. You are taking responsibility for what you really want. You're being responsible for being a leader through personal leadership. This mindset is the first part of shifting the paradigm to the new model of leadership. The second phase is recognizing that there is a version of you that lives irresponsibly – that is whole, complete and powerful. This version of you can produce at a high level and dent the universe in a big way. "Leadership is a State of Being" is about going into the future to learn about that version of yourself, and reverse-engineering what you see into the present.

This process can be likened to method acting, where an actor endeavors to have complete emotional identification with a character. It essentially is the art of finding the character within you and allowing yourself to be that. It's more like character embodiment than it is acting. I want you to embody and live your full potential.

You are the KPI.

As a leader, YOU are the #1 KPI in your life, your organization and your legacy. It is clearer than ever that the biggest factor for growing a business, or movement is growing the leader at the forefront of it. In order to fulfill your vision with the highest probability of transformation at a deep level, you need to expand more than ever before. Boldly embrace your ability to expand, and let's put a stop to this era of leadership where you get left out of the impact you're so desperately trying to have in the world.

The telltale signs of playing small (below your full potential) are unhappiness and depression. There are two big reasons why people feel bad: because you're inside a box that's stifling your potential and it's painful, or because you know that you could be somewhere else that's better. If you feel there is nothing left, you have an opportunity to discover the parts of yourself that you've been unwilling or unable to see.

Lead yourself first. This is not a war cry or declaration, it's about honoring the call echoing through that quiet storm of creative avoidance where you are ceaselessly pursuing financial success in lieu of legacy. Potential is about answering the call of desire – the call of expansion seeking to express itself. It is who you are.

It's impossible to low-level yourself to operate at a high

level. There is no amount of medium-level business or financial drive that you can take on to get you to high level. It doesn't work that way. In a sense, you have to burn everything down and leave it completely in order to open up the space required to get to the next level. After years as a successful coach who had created the lifestyle in Santa Barbara, I left everything I had built, burning it to the ground, because two items cannot occupy the same space at the same time.

It took courage to be bold enough to go for what I wanted. There was no road map for it, and no one else had ever really done it. In this expansion process, the more dimensions I was willing to look at in myself, the better; and the more depth I was willing to create in each one of those dimensions, the better. Ultimately, that season of change allowed me to be a more complete version of myself, so I was able to bring more of myself to the work of helping others expand. On the biggest scale, that showed up as even greater courage and more creativity.

Within a few short months of stepping into my own ideal potential, I had gone from getting paid for my knowledge and my experience (being paid to answer questions that I knew the answers to), to working with people to help them answer questions to which answers didn't yet exist. In my full potential, I was getting paid for my creativity and imagination. The shift happened because I trusted myself enough to go deep on the areas that I have avoided and be honest about what was holding me back from operating at my best.

You need to know how to identify what you really want – what is in alignment with the expanded game and the best version of yourself. Why? Because when you put a stake in the ground to claim a new way of operating, the result is that you are going to be almost instantly flooded with opportunities…but here's the catch: most opportunities are just distractions in disguise. These other options are most often safer, more convenient and easier to test your resolve; though, ultimately, they are designed to see how much you want the thing you say you want, and if you are willing to create the behavior and identity to live it out. This scenario wasn't new to me, and it has happened with almost all the people I work with, because at some point, they all wanted to play at an expanded level.

Are you ready to play at an expanded level?

Start with Why, then Ask Who

Think about what you have, what you do and who you are. Now think about what you *want to* have, do and be. What is the difference? Is the path that you are on taking you where you want to go? Are you living in alignment with your full potential? If not, what needs to change?

Simon Sinek has made us all aware that it is important to

Start with Why to gain clarity of the cause, belief or purpose that drives our business. Finding our why stops short of the complete question, which is "Who?" Our "Why" is very powerful, though discovering who you truly are and who you can be adds exponential dimension. Passion becomes your "Why" and your potential is the "Who."

Discovering who you truly are
and who you can be adds
exponential dimension.

Albert Einstein said, "You cannot solve your problems with the same level of thinking used to create them." Truer words have never been spoken. If there is a difference between the reality you currently live in and the grand vision you have to create (your legacy), *you are what needs to change.* There can be no difference in who you are compared to who you want to be in order to bring your dream into reality. This means the absolute best thing for you to do is to get total clarity on what that difference is between your current and ideal potential. In a sense, you reverse engineer the future version of yourself to be able to understand your future self's:

- Identity
- Beliefs
- Thoughts
- Feelings
- Actions

If you get still and quiet, you can open yourself up to seeing that future version of yourself. You can hear them and feel what it is like to be them. Ideally, you can interview them. From the top down, what are the identity, beliefs and thoughts, feelings and actions you need to adopt that are different than what you're currently doing? How can you learn from the future you? How can you extract some of what you've learned and implement it into who you are right now?

It is impossible to change any type of external or internal result without changing the subsequent identity, beliefs, thoughts and feelings directly associated to creating that result. Identity is at the top of the chain because identity drives behavior. Your decision-making process has everything to do with who you believe you are the most fundamental level. Your morals, values standards and expectations are guiding your every moment. Attempting to change behavior without changing the identity is like changing the wheels on a car with a flat tire without filling up the empty tank of gas. The external esthetics have changed, but the car goes nowhere.

The Personal Development Journey

There exists a preconception that the journey from feeling incomplete, insignificant and unworthy to feeling whole is complicated, when in reality, it's not. It doesn't have to be hard, cathartic, or part of an exhaustive therapy session. It can be simple. The preconception presumes that there are things about you that are missing. If you don't feel worthy, then there are things that you must do, be, get or have to make you worthy. All of these point to external solutions to an internal problem. As we covered in "Excellent vs. Non-excellent Drivers," an internal problem can only be solved with an internal solution.

When you go within for answers, you discover that you can never be more significant than you already are.

When you make the choice to go within for answers, what you discover (when you strip away all of the illusion of false stories and beliefs that don't serve you) is that you can never be more significant than you already are. You can never be more worthy or complete. This is the quantum perspective, the exponential perspective.

The best example may be when a child first comes into the world. They get 100% of their parents' love, unconditionally, just for existing. What that tells us is that worthiness is present from day one. A child does not need to perform, produce or achieve anything to be worthy. They are worthy by being who they already are. If that's true for one child, it's true for all children.

Why then should that be any different for adults?

What happens as we get older is that we cover up or mask who we truly are and who we can be, and we no longer believe that being ourselves is enough. The continuum of worthiness is not intended to break as we get older, though it occurs. Why? Because culturally, we take on illusionary beliefs and stories about our worthiness. We allow these stories to cover up our potentiality; and as a result, there is no shift, no change and no forward progress.

You can pick up a hundred-dollar bill and feel like it's not worth $100. You can look at it and say, "I think this is really only worth a dollar," but the belief doesn't change the actual worth. Worthiness, significance and all the major things that you that think you need to be able to feel complete already exist inside of you. Our value comes from ourselves, not from anything external. The sun does not power itself from external sources. It gives everything life, but the sun's life comes from the sun. It is a self-perpetuating energy machine, and we are the same. We trick ourselves into thinking that we're like the things that are dependent on the sun for energy, when in reality *we are the sun*. It's simply a matter of returning to the radiance and value within ourselves –

returning to that source of completeness. To intentionally have happiness, fulfillment and expansion built into your life directly influences your impact and your organization.

What are your practices or rituals for expansion – for moving into the best version of yourself?

If you're not clear about what your practices or rituals are, then get clear on what they are and then engage with them. Again, the expansion and innovation of an organization is only relative to the expansion of the founder.

The shift of the new era is about creating a revolution in our priorities, and gaining the understanding that *you come first*, that you matter. Everything changes when you change the way you see yourself. Once you realize that you are the sun, there isn't anything that you need, which opens you to live from a place of want. The sun naturally wants to expand its shine, but it doesn't need to – it wants to, as an extension of being complete within itself. When you live from a place where you don't need anything, but you want things, the game changes, because desire is expansion seeking to express itself. The need is different when it comes from being whole and complete, and so is the way you define and perceive your own identity.

The Role of Identity

What if I told you that you aren't going to get anything from this book?

You read that right.

What if instead, this book takes something away from you?

For people like you and me, clarity is essential.

100% of what you need to expand, fully realize your potential and live a legacy *already exists inside you.*

The challenge in gaining clarity is that you are standing in your own way.

This is not about vision boards or cookie-cutter blueprints.

This is about being pushed to dream bigger than ever before, to experience grace and ease, and to be the best version of yourself.

When you have arrived, you'll have shed all that is not you.

Emboldened and clear you will go forth on a path of simple, yet universal denting impact.

Results are important in any aspect of life, however when it comes to creating results whether that is increasing the bottom line, creating culture or changing the world there is a misconception of the most effective way to move the needle forward. At the top of the hierarchy of creation is identity. Imagine two people both desire a healthy and fit body. One believes that fitness is not something you do it is something you are, the other believes that working out and eating right is a chore. Which one do you think goes to the gym five days a week without fail? Which one fuels their body with organic vegetables? A new sexy body is on the top of most peoples list of achievements in the new year and by the end of March (if that long), the vast majority of those people have fallen off the wagon and never get back on. Why? Identity. Their actions are not connected to their identity.

The expansion process has to be initiated by a fundamental identity shift, because results are driven by behavior, and behavior is driven by identity. By fundamentally changing our identity, there is a trickle-down effect of behavior, and ultimately results. There must be a willingness on your part to understand this effect and to be able to go into your soul about it. Going that deep within – into the multiple dimensions of who you are – helps you realize what is about to happen. It helps you realize what *can* happen when you apply the identity-development and quantum leap that this book is about. The difference that will be created for you and for your organization is immeasurable.

An individual can change everything on the outside – new gym clothes, a gym membership and some vegetables sitting in the fridge – but if they don't change, nothing else will. They have to *become the person* who *goes* to the gym and *eats* the vegetables. This is, of course, a metaphor for leadership.

All the results a leader desires to experience from themselves and others must start at the level of identity. We see this all the time in the corporate world, where hundreds of billions of dollars are spent each year on workshops, training, speakers and consultants. While this is "good," it's a far-cry from "great" because, by-and-large, the employees don't need more information – they need an embodied example that leads to transformation. If you are seeking internal growth for your organization, doesn't it make sense for that growth to come not only from within, but also from the visionary leading the charge? Leaders need to lead themselves and others first. The change you desire is your responsibility to create, and if you want the highest probability of that change A) happening and B) lasting a long time it is best for you to be the source or it rather than an advocate of it. It must stem from your identity.

From a culture perspective, this completely changes the game. At a high level, you impart onto your team the key traits that make a difference. They build character on top of skill. This allows them to not only be empowered by the company's vision, it also gives them greater power in creating it. Their job then breaches far beyond something they clock in and out of, to become something that is a part of who they are. The end user also becomes included, as they feel that by using your product or service, not only do they get the benefits of what you are offering, they get to be a part of something bigger than themselves. Their identity shifts to someone who is a supporter and promoter of what it is you stand for. This is the essence of building a legacy.

Whatever you're building or creating, or movement you're leading, the dent you're making in the universe is a form of self-expression. The highest form of self-expression occurs when your identity is expressed through what you do, rather than what you do defining who you are. There is a big difference, and that means things could radically change, but *you* don't change. In an era where everything is changing so rapidly, having a solid, certain sense of who you are is key. There is so much uncertainty in the world right now – some of it scary, and some of it exciting. What must not be uncertain at any step of the way is your identity and your purpose: who you are and why you're here. If those things are unshakeable, you will be able to weather the storm and to be, do, have and give everything you want.

If your identity and purpose are unshakeable, you will be able to weather the storm.

What is Identity?

At the deepest level, your identity is your potential. Who we are is what we are, and what we are is our potential…and that potential is limitless. Your identity has everything to do with who and what you *are*, not what you do. That's the fundamental disconnect: most people believe their identity is what they do or is some function of what they do. We believe that we are successful because of external things. In the Western world, we are measured by our roles: what we produce, and what (or how much) we have – things you can see or have proof of. You are not your performance, your production, or your title. None of those things are our identity. They are limiting and tangible, while your identity is not. Other than your physical body, 100% of who you are is invisible. You can't touch it or see it. Isn't funny to think that the most valuable and rich parts of life are unable to be seen?

This new era of leadership comes with an understanding of what your identity is at the most fundamental level; at a level of unconditional love and worthiness. It is a state of being. Your identity has more to do with your essence and values. It has more to do with art than it does with science. It has more to do with things that are invisible than those that are tangible. Your identity has to do with passion and purpose. It has to do with what you believe is beautiful and magical in the world.

When you challenge yourself to see yourself as bigger than what you have been, what do you see?

If you are defined by your role and lose your role, who are you? If you are defined by what you produce or how much you have and all of that changes, what happens to your identity? When you remove these external components you considered your identity, what's left? This happens all the time to people with amazing careers. They lose their job and experience an "identity crisis." A founder can experience the same with a big exit from their company. They think they'll live "the good life," but they don't know how to be in the world without their company, because their company became their identity.

The new era model recognizes that our identity (and the development of our identity) is comprised of two things: our potential and our purpose.

Identity = Potential + Purpose

The first piece of your identity is who you are beyond all titles and achievements. The second piece is your purpose. Your purpose is not your role; your purpose is why you're here. Through the course of your lifetime, it may look very different over the years. It may take on different forms and shapes, yet, at its core, your purpose remains the same. Like an actor plays different characters in movies—they can be a bad guy, a good guy, a joker, a king—their purpose remains to be an actor and to entertain.

One of our major purposes is the same from person to person, which is to make the world a better place. I believe we all, in some way, shape, or form, want to make the world a better place. In our hierarchy of needs, we all have a desire to be part of something that's bigger than ourselves. If that wasn't part of our purpose, and if purpose wasn't part of our identity, why would that be inserted into the code of who we are? At the most microscopic level of our DNA, why would that be coded into us? Self-actualization stands at the peak of Maslow's hierarchy of needs for a reason: it is not optional. Living true to our full potential is necessary to live a powerful and fulfilled life. Everything on that hierarchy of needs is important, especially being part of something bigger than yourself.

The journey to self-actualization will look and feel different for every person because we are individuals. At the highest point of realized needs, we all become artists, and the lens through which we view the world and our desire for fulfillment is the point from where the paint comes out. It's where the beauty comes out. The way you want to impact the world is different than how I want to do it, but it comes from the same place. We both have that same innate desire to paint a picture of a better world. Our work will come out looking very different, but the pieces come from the same sense of identity we each have, which is a sense of being who we are.

What do you stand for?

What do you believe in?

What is your purpose?

When a painter comes to the crossroads headlined by the question "to paint or not paint," what are they going to choose? They are going to paint, because that's what painters are intended to do. The challenge, again, is that too many of us put ourselves in a box. When the opportunity comes to expand – to do something bigger than yourself – you are not conditioned to do it. When a painter sells themselves on the idea that *not* painting is a good idea, they experience pain and suffering. When you cut off *any* of our human needs, you are making the decision that being part of something bigger than yourself isn't a priority. Without indulging in your desires (expansion seeking to express itself) and questioning our own potentiality, you stifle yourself and your identity.

Removing Limiting Beliefs

The challenge with growth and next-level expansion is that

most people feel like they will acquire something in the process to make them worthier, more capable or more significant. At the highest level, transformation and growth is much more a subtractive process than additive one. To embrace the things that you have to be more of, you need only own those parts of yourself. In order for you to be less of things that are holding you back, you need to let go of those things. It is only when you subtract everything that is in the way of living your potential that you expand. It has to do with removing the illusion that is keeping you from the truth.

The expansion process is a function of two things, but most people have them backward:

1. Removing the limiting beliefs and stories that you've bought into either from other people or from yourself that cause you to believe that you're not good enough. Once those are removed, then you have a clean slate that you then can take onto part two:

2. Reaching a point of feeling whole, complete and worthy, and asking yourself what beliefs, skills, abilities, traits and identities do you need to take on to really elevate your game.

These two steps allow you to build from an excellent foundation, rather than trying to add excellent components on a non-excellent foundation. The biggest step of clarification is asking if there are beliefs you have that are preventing you from expanding. If there are, shift them. Beliefs are made up – created in the mind – so just because you currently believe something doesn't mean that you always have believed that, or that you need to believe it going forward. Either your belief came from an outside source, or you came to some conclusion on your own. Regardless of whether the belief is true or not, you now get to decide if the belief is going to support you.

Letting go of old beliefs means realizing that they may have served a purpose at one point in time, but now do not. There is a fable of the guy who was flying a helicopter over the jungle when his helicopter crashed. He had to get to the next town over to find safety, but there's a big river standing between him and his destination. He couldn't cross it, because it's too deep and it's too fast. So, he made a raft with his machete and nearby bamboo trees. When he gets safely across the river, he's so happy, because without the raft, he wouldn't have been able to make it. Because the raft was so beneficial, he keeps it – putting it on his back and carrying it with him. He feels attached to it. A few miles ahead, trying to get through the jungle becomes increasingly strenuous with the heavy raft weighing him down. It is then that he comes to the conclusion that there are no more rivers that he needs to cross, and he can let the raft go.

Our beliefs are not our identity, our beliefs are just a function of something we created in our minds to serve us at one point in time. Sometimes even limiting beliefs serve us. They can validate us or keep us safe in some way. In order to shift them or let them go, we have to reach a point where we realize we don't need them anymore. You have to reach a place where you accept the fact that if you continue holding onto a certain limiting belief, it's going to be detrimental – it's going to keep you from getting what you want and realizing your full potential.

What are your limiting beliefs costing you?

The second part of the process is about embracing – creating new beliefs that are the vehicle to make this reality that you desire possible and elevate your game. If you want to create the highest probability of realizing your full potential and ultimate vision of reality, then it's your responsibility to embrace that belief. All beliefs are just like muscles. The more you practice them, the better you get.

Development =
Character + Gravity of Decision

When it comes to discovering and developing our identity, there is an important distinction that needs to be made between principles and development. Principles are concepts you pick up and put down as required. The reason principles are not long-term is because there typically isn't gravity in the decision to which they are tied. For instance, New Year's resolutions can be considered principles – people may apply them and then drop them, and they typically don't last. Development, at the highest level, is about your character and identity. It something that you either are or are not, and therefore cannot be picked up or dropped. The second aspect to development is that it is based on gravity of decision. When you decide to develop, there is no going back. Expansion, for instance, is a natural part of who you are, and once you grow into a more expanded version of yourself, the advancement cannot be undone.

Principles and strategies apply to the current game – the one-dimensional, bottom-line-driven model of leadership – yet they do not guarantee that anything changes, at the most fundamental or global level. There is no gravity of decision, nor is there necessarily a fit between a principle that has worked for someone else and what will work for you. Why have other leadership principles and strategies not worked to create happiness and fulfillment for you? Because you can't just do what someone else did and expect the same result. There must be development of character in order to fully embody whatever it was that this other person it did. To guarantee change, you need to focus on development, or "quantum principles." Principles only work when you embody them as part of multidimensional development.

The title words we attach to our identity are very limited: mom, dad, doctor, business owner, founder, achiever, etc. They are not false, though they are also not complete because they have limits. As soon as you apply terms and roles to your identity, there are conditions...and those conditions tend to be quite restrictive. Part of the awakening process is understanding that your identity has nothing to do with your role in your relationships, your family, in your community, your title at your job, or your performance. All of the things we typically associate our identity with are substitutes for what your identity actually is. Our identity is so much deeper and vivid and full of life than the words we attach to it. It comes from your relation to yourself, your understanding of yourself. It has nothing to do with anything external, because as soon as it does, you limit your limitless potential and completely misunderstand who you are at a fundamental level.

Are you okay just being you?

When you strip away your desire to race towards an end goal, and strip down your identity to its most raw form, can you exist in this space and be okay with who you are? If you want to constantly race and drive, it is difficult to just sit in this space. It feels like a void, because your value, significance and identity have always come from performance and production. To have an identity defined by your potential and your purpose allows you to create from who you are, rather than forcing yourself to adopt something that isn't who you are. Purpose and potential must be part of how you live and breathe in the world, because they are the foundation of what makes you a leader.

Surfing the Void

When your worth is unshakeable, you're willing to take greater risks.

You'll fail more too.

And yet with a deep sense of self-appreciation the failure doesn't phase you.

You have one purpose in life, and that is to expand.

It's the mistrust of that infinite self that prevents us from growing.

That stagnation at the highest level is true failure.

A deep knowing must be reached that is the absolute truth of who you are: Unconditional love.

Nothing to fear, nothing to lose.

Leaping into and through the void is a process of development.

You are a blank canvas waiting to be filled with the meaning. In order to live your full potential, you must detach from your limited one-dimensional definitions of who you are and embrace the limitless, expanded version of yourself. Taking this quantum leap matters greatly in your pursuit of leadership.

The lyrics of Pink Floyd's "Wish you were here" ask, "Did they get you to trade your heroes for ghosts? Hot ashes for trees? Hot air for a cool breeze? Cold comfort for change? And did you exchange, a walk on part in the war for a lead role in a cage?" To become an irresponsible, expanded leader, it's going to take a good amount of courage because you're going to depart from belief systems and most likely parts of your identity. It's a challenging process because you've spent years developing an identity that is an illusion, which has caused you great suffering. Even the best identity created in a linear, one-dimensional place cannot serve our multidimensional existence.

Even the best identity created in a linear, one-dimensional place cannot serve your multidimensional existence.

The shift of the new era of leadership requires that you leave behind things that are comfortable or familiar to you and discover things that feel completely irresponsible or identities that were initially unrelatable to you. You will feel a whole myriad of feelings ranging from fear to uncertainty. There will inevitably come a point where you come to the conclusion that all the things you think you are go away…and yet, you haven't fully embraced the truest version of what your identity is. You'll be in between – in the void.

In a world that thrives on certainty, making a quantum leap often requires finding yourself in the exact opposite. Jeff Bezos is a great example of this. Leaping from his job at a New York hedge fund, he humbly began Amazon.com out of his garage in Seattle. In just over two decades, he became the richest man on the planet.[28] Imagine how many major shifts happened internally for him – beliefs, thoughts, feelings and his identity all undoubtedly changed. Without a doubt, there were times where he was in-between versions of himself. In order to become the man behind the largest online shopping retailer, he had to accept a revolution of self. The change was notable from the outside, with early pictures showing him baggy clothes with silly smile, transforming into current-day snapshots of him in a fitted polo shirt and vest showing his rugged biceps. Of course, it is likely that the biggest changes have happened from the inside out.

Surfing the Void

The void can be a scary place to be, because it means not being in motion if you are someone who is accustomed to being in motion. This phase is what I call "surfing the void" – the space

---

[28] http://time.com/money/4746795/richest-people-in-the-world/

where you're in between certainties. You are certain of what you already know (i.e. things that are familiar or comfortable to you), but there are other things you want to be certain of (i.e. what the future will look and feel like) and you aren't there yet. When you've let go of what you know and who you thought you were, you find yourself in midair, moving toward what's uncertain in the hopes that it will become certain. You're not quite able to reach either certainty. Surfing the void with grace requires you to remain calm, cool and collected in that moment. What happens if you lean too far forward on a surfboard when you're in a wave? You bail. What happens if you lean too far back? You bail. You've got to be balanced. You have to be willing to be *fully* in the void. Do not try to do anything other than be in the moment.

Surfing the void is not for the weak of heart. It requires serious courage because you for a time lose yourself. It is one thing to learn how to detach from things; it is completely different to detach from who you are. Doing so can only happen with a deep level of trust. This trust in a deeper/higher version of ourselves – a version that is stronger and more capable than the last – is faith that who you've been is not the peak of who you are and that your greatest achievements are not behind you. As uncertain as the void can be, it is essential to intentionally step into it.

The greatest growth opportunity in creating a bigger dent in the universe will always be to go within and step into "the internal unknown." From there, any external uncharted territory can be pursued with fearlessness. Going from the known to the unknown is the most quintessential leap of faith of all. There has to be a willingness to be courageous enough to know that what you are feeling and experiencing are worth it. You have to believe in what is on the other side: the version of you that is whole. The expanded version of you can lead, create and develop an organization that has depth and innovation, and is based on trust and collaboration. One of the biggest pre-qualifiers is that you have the courage to be able to become that person.

The leap takes a different amount of time for every person, but one factor remains consistent: for a period of time you have no identity. The pain, depression, and sadness that come along with being in the void are, in many ways, a version of ourselves that most people are unwilling to experience. There is a gap in your capacity and your ability – a discomfort you have to be willing to sit in. It's a painful process to go through. Becoming the expanded leader is a journey only for those who are willing to embark on something that requires a level of boldness. To be in a void where you have not fully embraced the truest version of yourself can make you feel lost, when in reality, you are in perfect alignment with where you need to be.

Why do we leap into the void?

You leap because you know it's only for a season. Knowing the uncertainty, pain and discomfort will pass is how you navigate the void powerfully. Continue to have a clear vision of what you want. This doesn't mean you're not going to feel all the emotions that come along with the ride; but you know there's light at the end of the tunnel. The light is what gave you the courage to jump in the first place; and it will give you the fortitude to put in the work and stay in it long enough to get to the other side.

How do you realize who you are – limitless in potential and purpose?

What are the tools required to redefine identity and navigate the void?

Diving into Worthiness

The void is the best place to work on your worthiness. The void is a little unforgiving, in a way. There is nothing else to do but work on your sense of worth. Having chosen to leap into the void, you cannot go back to who you were. Like having departed from a planet, you're now in the in-between. The next destination is one that you can't go to yet, so you just have to sit with yourself in the void. Be without angst to go back or be at the destination.

Determining what you desire has moved you ahead, away from the old achievement-driven model of leadership. Reverse-engineering the ideal of your future, full-potential self has painted the picture of where you are going. While lingering between these two known points, it can feel like you are not achieving...though let me reassure you, what you are undertaking it the greatest revolution of self that you will ever know. Like a magnet drawing two poles together, you are working on making sense on all that you have been and all that you will be.

You are undertaking the greatest revolution of self you will ever know.

You can't revolutionize yourself if you can't sit still in the void and be okay with being you. Happiness is self-acceptance. It's hard to have happiness any other way. Self-acceptance comes first, and the ability to find beauty in the moment comes second. To be able to fall in love with the moment, whatever the moment is offering to you, is beautiful, especially in the transformative nature of the void.

The first practice in the void is to be okay with not doing anything, knowing that you are in fact doing some of the more critical "work" you will ever do. In the void, your existence is no longer validated with manic, frantic action. You have to overcome your addiction to whatever is beyond the present moment. Realize that the moment is good enough, that it is not something you have to get beyond to get to something else that will make you feel a certain way. The second practice is determining whether, without external roles, titles or performance to tie your identity to, you can be okay with your worth.

Center yourself into your feelings of being enough. You are worthy of all abundance. In the past, you may have wanted that external validation to feel whole and complete. It was much like trying to fill a bucket that's got a hole in the bottom. The void is where everything changes – where you learn to feel whole, complete and give from a full cup. The void is where you come to know that you are enough just as you are...and that awareness leads to a revolution of self.

Revolution of Self

The process of discovering our worthiness is one of the most powerful endeavors a person can go on, because most people struggle with the idea of not being enough. On the other end of the spectrum lies this idea that you are more than enough just as you are. You don't need to achieve, strive, hustle, grind, win, prove or dent the universe to validate this worthiness. You can be content, be one with God and be happy, just as you are. There is nothing more to it than that. Own your worth and your passion. Let yourself feel how good it feels to come to the conclusion that you're already as worthy as you can be, you're already as significant as you can ever be.

You're already as significant as you can ever be.

This is the place from which we build the new era of leadership – where you enable yourself to expand. From this place, you remember that your worthiness has always been there, in one form or another. It's time to give yourself permission to make this journey from unworthiness, insignificance or inadequate to whole, complete and limitless.

The Void + Revolution of Self = Embodied Leadership

The result of allowing yourself to be in the void and experience a revolution of self is that you come to fully embody leadership. The pinnacle of the expanded leader is the place where you can be certain that you are more than enough as you are. At this ultimate point, you also know that you don't need to achieve or have accolades to realize your value. From there, you get to go, achieve, create and make a dent the universe, because you are enough, *because* you are happy...not because you need to become happy. You are giving from a place of being whole and complete.

The expanded leader steps into a totally different paradigm, knowing that because you are full means you get to expand. The expansion process does not end when you become a whole, complete leader.

Embodied Leadership

The depth of your impact is directly related to the depth of your magic.

You either have a gift or you are a gift.

With being a gift comes a call.

A sense of duty to be a servant leader and a major cause with the effect of global change.

More than anything it comes with a strong desire to help others.

The absolute most important thing you can do is to constantly and neverendingly refine and perfect your alchemy – the ability to change what you see before you.

Think of yourself as a magician.

You have the ability to turn lead into bronze.

What if you could also turn lead into silver? Silver into gold?

Being a gift is not a process of adding more skills.

If anything, it is a process of stripping away everything that is in the way of the most potent version of you and your gift.

Let's explore, let's pioneer, the vastness of you and the frontier you are destined to discover.

Let's reveal the leader within.

Leadership is a state of being – an identity rather than an action or role. It has no dollar value, corporate title or level of achievement as a point of entry, because it is not something that you do…it is something that you are. It is not about your idea, your product or having a gift. There are people in the world who, from an achievement or financial standpoint, have nothing or next to nothing, yet are happy and fulfilled. Why? Because their sense of identity, purpose, and drive has nothing to do with proving. It has nothing to do with filling a void they are incapable or unwilling to fill themselves. Leadership, like identity, does not come from titles or achievement; it is who you are when all else is stripped away.

Leadership is not something that you do, it is something that you are.

The concept of being a leader of an organization when you go to work, and when you leave, you're not, is absurd. If you're a leader, then you're a leader. A true leader lives in integrity with the qualities of great leadership wherever you are. The new era is about transcending into an identity of leadership, so that in all of your behavior and in all moments – whether at home, by yourself, with friends or family, or at the grocery store – you are embodying the qualities of leadership. The boldness, compassion, innovation and power that you bring to embarking on the impossible in business is maintained whether you are doing the dishes, hanging out with your kids, going to the gym, attending church, or whatever your days entail. Leadership breathes throughout your entire life, because it is who you are.

Embodied leadership means that you appreciate and innovate yourself by improving and expanding your capacity. It creates a very different path for getting from where you are to where you want to be.

Client Story

Cam Adair is doing something that no one has done before – something that is making a huge difference in the world. As the founder of Game Quitters, he and his team help members in 85 countries, to the sum of 50,000 people a month, quit their addiction to video games. The business has doubled in past year and Cam was named one of Canada's "Top Under-50 Leaders in Mental Health." Despite exposure in major media platforms, he will be the first to tell you that it's about the lives that are changed through his vision.

Every day, he and his team receive letters from members telling them how they can relate to Cam's personal story of video game addiction. Is it not unheard of for Game Quitters being credited with helping a member avert suicide. The deep impact of Cam's work happens because he is willing to let his end users and team know that he was just like them. He uses the power of story to change people's lives.

When Cam and I began working together, he was burnt out and his personal life was suffering. The paradigm being shifted for all of you who feel or have felt like him is to have everything come back into balance. As he says, "Our impact is limited by our own self-care."

In order to have the impact that you want to have, and help as many people as possible, you have to take care of yourself and give from a full cup. Embodying deep leadership means that you feel whole and are not willing to sacrifice yourself...and yet, you're willing to do whatever is necessary to move your vision forward. For Cam, this include following "his highest excitement," or the passions that brought him the greatest happiness. Sometimes this meant surfing, other times it was engaging in meaningful conversation...and more often than not, the greatest thing that he could do for himself was sleep.

When you are doing something that has never been done

before – being creative, innovative and resourceful while venturing into the unknown – you have to be operating from a full cup and living true to what you want.

What Cam discovered in his quest to expanded leadership was that he was not doing his best while working in the operating side of the business. He brought in a partner and was able to step out of his own way. That partner stepped forward, giving him freedom to dedicate himself to his passions for speaking, bringing awareness, and being in the media sharing the powerful articulation of his cause.

Leadership can sometimes be about getting out of your own way. Be responsible for your genius. The more powerfully Cam showed up, the more difference that made for everyone else. So often, the focus is on the vision, and not on who you have to become in order to share that vision with deep impact. It always has to be about the quality of time you are spending, not the quantity.

When asked how he defines leadership, Cam said, "When I think of leadership, I think of vulnerability…going first and making your experiences transparent." By creating a more holistic approach to his life (following his highest excitement), he now embodies leadership and shows others that the same is possible for them. There is a ripple effect, whereby the leader's being responsible has created a culture within Game Quitters where the people are invested in seeing the community and cause go forward (instead of focusing on getting video game addiction help for themselves and then leaving). Everyone is giving from a full cup, embodying leadership.

Since the day Cam wrote the first blog post on the topic of healing video game addiction, the energy around Game Quitters for him and his team has been about taking a stand and saying "we're going forward." He was no longer willing to accept video game addiction as part of our reality, and he took responsibility for doing something about it. However, he is not looking to do it alone; he's looking to do it "together, in arms."

The embodied leader infuses a sense of responsibility and desire to become a part of something bigger than themselves within every aspect of their organization and vision. They enroll people in cultivating a greater sense of impact, moving beyond the pain anyone is experiencing on a micro level.

Becoming aware of whether you embody leadership at the highest level means observing yourself and the way others react to you. Do you feel in integrity with the principles, ideas, visions, morals and standards that you project to the world (or not)? Is the feedback you get from others telling you that you are in alignment with the things you are saying you align with? Do you embody leadership? Do you walk your talk?

Do you walk your talk?

There are two questions to measure if are you walking your talk: How do you feel if you're really honest about who you are? What do other people say about you? If you're not in alignment, not quite there yet, you continue in development. If you're not walking your talk then what is the mindset, what is the habit, what is the thing preventing you from doing so? If you're not being completely in alignment and integrous with your embodiment of leadership, there is usually a belief creating a "conflicting reality," meaning that you say you want one thing, but have beliefs that are contrary. In order to fully expand and embody leadership, you need to shift the limiting belief or habit.

Saying that a leader is someone who is fully expressed and lives in the full realization of their potential means you embrace all of the dimensions of the expanded leader because you know that is who you are. The art of fulfillment is based on the full self-expression and multidimensional expansion of the leader. If you're going to be a complete leader, a whole leader, expansion must occur in all directions: expansion of the depths of yourself; understanding and accepting yourself; challenging yourself; growing all aspects of yourself, your personal life and your spiritual life – all of the pieces of the puzzle. Expansion is, to this new era leader, a diverse perspective. It is most definitely not linear or one-dimensional.

The value of constantly expanding has been demonstrated in places like Japan, where this idea of kaizen, or continuous "change for the better," is at the forefront of how they do things. However, the fact that Japan has the third-highest suicide rates in the world[29] emphasizes the point that continuous improvement alone is not enough – it needs to be multidimensional. There must be fulfillment in all areas of our lives. Has the Japanese culture swung the pendulum so far into excellence in production that they've forgotten about happiness and fulfillment? People are so overworked in Japan that they are literally dying on their train ride home from exhaustion.

Japan is a micro version of a macro problem. For decades, Gallup has been measuring international employee satisfaction. Their study shows only 13% of employees worldwide are engaged in their jobs. 63% are "not engaged" and 24% are "actively disengaged."[30] These numbers are both staggering and 100% unnecessary. Let's get real. We are talking about millions upon millions of people who are hating, or at very best displeased with, their jobs.

What measures did Gallup used to reach these conclusions? These 12 questions to assess employee happiness[31] serve as a

[29] http://www.bbc.com/news/world-33362387
[30] http://news.gallup.com/businessjournal/188033/worldwide-employee-engagement-crisis.aspx
[31] http://news.gallup.com/businessjournal/162041/applying-employee-engagement-specific-business-problem.aspx

valuable reference point for all of us to gauge our happiness:

1. I know what is expected of me at work.
2. I have the material and equipment I need to do my work right.
3. At work, I have the opportunity to do what I do best every day.
4. In the last seven days, I have received recognition or praise for doing good work.
5. My superior, or someone at work, seems to care about me as a person.
6. There is someone at work who encourages my development.
7. At work, my opinions seem to count.
8. The mission or purpose of my company makes me feel my job is important.
9. My associates or fellow employees are committed to doing quality work.
10. I have a best friend at work.
11. In the last six months, someone at work has talked to me about my progress.
12. This last year, I have had opportunities to learn and grow.

Go deep on leadership parts for each of these. When there is a commitment to expansion, you create an ever-improving product and a better end-user experience. Couple that with personal fulfillment and happiness, and you've created something that's exponentially beneficial. You are then playing an exponential game and everyone from the top-level executives and janitor, to the end user, can feel it.

Embodying expanded leadership means that you understand the importance of adapting every dimension of what it is to be a healthy, happy, fulfilled leader now. If it isn't important to you now, it most likely won't be later. Behavior is a function of identity, and if your identity now is that of someone who is sacrificing things like health, relationships, or your own happiness and fulfillment, in the name of validation, markers and financial achievement, you are not going to find fulfillment.

Do you embody a leader who is expanding in multiple dimensions?

What is the result of embodying multidimensional expansion?

The Deep Leader

The result of multidimensional expansion is the creation of a deep, whole and complete leader. You are willing to bring the absolute best of yourself (your full potential) to the table. Doing so happens because you feel complete. You feel whole and are not willing to sacrifice yourself...and yet, you're willing to do whatever is necessary to make your dent in the universe and leave a legacy. This journey creates an interesting paradigm, where you're not willing to sacrifice yourself (in the wrong ways), yet you are willing to be the sword and shield for other people. The level from which this occurs is more than most leaders have, because the deep leader is operating from overflow. They can do both and remain whole.

It's much more powerful to be a sword and shield for your people if you're in overflow than if you are not. Culturally, we have championed this idea of the martyr leader, which has become a gross misrepresentation of what an expanded leader should be. We're using examples of people like Mother Teresa – people who are completely misunderstood. Most people would say that she's an amazing leader, and she was; but she was also made out to be a bit of a martyr, because many people believed that she had no money. The perception was that she selflessly went where she needed to be to serve other people. Most people don't know that she had millions of dollars. She gave from a place of overflow and not from a place of emptiness.

Mother Teresa embodied deep leadership. Not only did she do a lot of what she did on her own, she also inspired other people within her "organization" to do the same thing. The echo of her work continues on to this day. In the new era of expanded leadership, we'll essentially have a whole group of modern Mother Teresas.

There is a difference between being a servant leader and sacrificing as a leader. The expanded leader does not involve sacrifice because you serve from a full cup. You have such a deep internal relationship that you trust yourself; you trust their own potential and capacity. This lends itself to trusting in the big picture, in the unknown, in things that you don't have control over…because you don't need to have control these things. You are able to do all of this because of a belief that the universe, God, or whatever you call the greater power, and knowing that power is really a mirror reflecting who you are.

You have what it takes to be a complete leader and to create something that massively impacts the world *without* having to sacrifice, having control everything or continuously being validated. Not only does this state of deep leadership take your ability to be, do, and give to a completely different level, but as a leader, it allows the people within your organization and people in the outside world to realize that a leader does not have to be a martyr. The expanded leader helps others realize that being full is the best place to give from. This will, in turn, inspire people within the organization to show up differently and not sacrifice themselves. Your choice to embody leadership at this level gives others a new and better paradigm from which to operate.

Depth in an organization, in a culture, is only possible based on the depth of the leader. The people in the organization can only follow the leader as deep as that leader is. Can you think of any companies that have amazing cultures with a non-excellent founder? There are not many, if not none at all, because the people in the organization ultimately don't follow the vision, they follow the visionary.

In the old tyrannical model, this following was fear-based; in the new era, people in the organization are a part of the vision because they feel connected to the leader – the depth of the leader – as someone they aspire to be around or to be like.

Are you living the boldness, courage and innovation of an expanded leader?

Is that essence a part of yourself, your organization and your impact?

What does it mean to be a great leader? There are plenty of books and methodologies that offer a dry, black-and-white, cookie-cutter framework that would have you adhere to a certain way of doing things...though as we covered, the old model creates a dangerous paradigm with the restrictive presumptions of how and what a leader should be. Being a great, expanded leader will not come by plugging into a pre-existing framework or formula. You have to find your unique way of being a leader – one that embodies your full self-expression and full expansion.

From there, you have to determine whether you have a gift or you are a gift, and how you will deliver that impact to make a dent in the universe.

Are You a Gift?

If I were to ask you whether you have a gift *or* you are a gift, what would you say? Many leaders, especially of companies with products, would probably believe they *have* a gift rather than thinking they *are* a gift, because what you are bringing to the world is your product, which is true. Consider this: the success of the company depends on the success of the leader, so in reality, you *are* a gift. In this new era, the leadership you bring forward is going to have the greatest impact on changing the world – the full expression of your full potential is going to create the shift from the old model of leadership to this new one. Your being a gift is what matters most in this equation.

How does it feel to be a gift and to be expanded?

To be a gift means that there is a positive shift in what other people experience when they are in your atmosphere. How do you determine that you are a gift? Making the determination of whether you are a gift means becoming aware of how people experience of you. What is their experience of you? Do they have a positive, powerful experience when they're around you? Not just on one occasion, but all the time.

It's important to understand that many leaders who really *are* a gift believe that they *have* a gift, which it what causes them to under appreciate themselves and seek validation. Most leaders have never considered the idea that they could *be* a gift – a single awareness that changes the game. You live your life thinking that you have a gift, and you try to figure out what that means and how you should show up in the world to offer your gift, when in reality, there is no seeking to reveal your gift, because you *are* a gift. Being able to differentiate between having and being allows you to say, "Even if I have a product to sell, the most valuable thing I'm bringing to the world is myself and my leadership." This perspective causes you to focus on completely different things.

It takes worthiness to accept that you are a gift. It is fundamentally different and feels different than worth that is driving from having a gift or creating a product. It's about the feeling that occurs when you don't have any tangible thing to give to the world and others are impact by solely your essence – your invisible identity. Stepping into the realization that you are a gift is as valuable as spearheading the invention of something as great as the iPhone. That's a hard pill to swallow if you don't feel worthy. You really have to be saturated into worthiness to be able to own the fact that you, in your essences, just as valuable as the invention of the iPhone. The void gifts you the space to step into that worthiness of being a gift. As tough as that may be to grasp I want you to play with it. It may not currently seem true, but HOW could it be true?

When you come to the conclusion that you are a gift, then the next question becomes: what is your gift?

What is your gift?

You get clear on what your gift is when you look at what people experience when they're with you. Do they feel safe? Do they feel motivated? Do they feel excited? Do they feel emboldened? Do they feel like they're part of something bigger than themselves? Your gift comes down to how do people respond to you when they are in your atmosphere. That's a big illuminator of what type of gift you have. For example, with indigo people, typically, most people in their atmosphere will feel very safe and trusting. These gifted individuals have a natural gift of helping others open up and tell them their life story or most intimate secrets, within five minutes of meeting. The particular way in which people respond to you points directly to something about your gift. Observe how others act or react toward you.

Great leaders, like Mother Theresa, were a gift, and that's why people followed them. That's why they were so great. The more worthy you feel, the more you can feel safe to leap into the impossible, to be irresponsible, to step into being a gift and to fully embody what it means to be a whole, complete leader. It is then that you have fully embraced the expansion process and leave your legacy and dent in the universe.

I believe there is a leader in all of us. Some say that there are people who are meant to follow and people who are meant to lead. I don't agree. There is no "leader" and "follower"; we all have the potential to be leaders. While it may look and feel different from person to person, or within the context of personal leadership, leadership is a part of all of us. This doesn't mean that you have to lead big movements or organizations; you only have to direct yourself in your own experience of life. The opportunity to live in full expression of ourselves and the full realization of our potential is yours to take.

Shannon Graham

NEW METRICS & MOTIVATORS

Shannon Graham

MYTH:

Leadership is for those at the top.

TRUTH:

Leaders create leaders organization-wide.

Revolution & Contribution

There must be an attachment to letting go of what is outdated.

As you grow, your value and ability grow.

Old systems and mindset are a reflection of who you were, not who you've become.

Go above your knowledge and experience, accessing your creativity and imagination.

Do what brings you the enjoyment you desire.

Add value to others and value to yourself.

Reach beyond the "good enough" level of development.

Awaken to your limitless potential and full expression.

This revolution of self will spell the end of the tyrant, one-dimensional leader.

None of us want to feel as though the dream of leadership has turned into a prison sentence. You want depth to your work and deep impact for your vision. Happiness and fulfillment have to be the focal point, as you come into the full expression of yourself and full realization of your potential. In the new era of expanded leadership, no longer are you as the leader being left out. As of right now, in a lot of ways, the reward for massive success is isolation, depression and unfulfillment. It's time to flip the switch and have fulfillment, connection and happiness exist from the onset. What happens when these metrics exist and only increase as time goes by? A total revolution of the game. Wouldn't you agree?

End of Productivity

No one needs to tell you about the current emphasis on productivity. Currently, and unfortunately, the metric for success in leadership is the bottom line of the business. Where the danger lies is that productivity can be mistaken or misguided into busyness and can overrule a happiness or value-oriented focus. Busyness is the enemy and the opposite of productivity, even though it can have some of the hallmarks of it. As the Navy SEALs say, "Slow is smooth and smooth is fast." If you ever watch how they move, it isn't fast, but it is smooth. They are very intentional. When shit hits the fan, and they're in the middle of it, they don't run, they drop their stance, drop their weight and move slowly but quickly. They engage their target and move through their target. Non-reactive, they do not feel the need to rise to the occasion; they default to their elite training.

This correlates to the activities that move the needle on performance: happiness, fulfillment and contribution – the metrics that matter. It means allowing ourselves to have all of these things. Bruce Lee is a great example of this, because he was one of the most revolutionary martial artists of all time, and also one of the most controversial. In the martial arts world, especially back in his day, each style was very particular to itself. If you did karate, then you didn't mix or have anything to do with Taekwondo. Creating those multiple dimensions would be like a devout Christian also getting into some Buddhism and mixing it with a little bit of Taoism. What Bruce Lee did wasn't acceptable to many, but he did it anyway. He moved the needle and redefined what he did well, which was fight. The guys he fought were primarily trained in only one discipline. When they came at him in a very linear way, he could adapt. If they were using their hands, he'd use feet. If he could tell they were going to use feet, he would take them to the ground. He was fluid, adaptable and smooth.

The expanded leader is equally fluid and adaptable, because you've made the choice to do away with the old one-dimensional model and the bottom-line focus that isn't truly moving the needle forward. Financial success can feel like it's the most important focus, but it's not. It is one of a diversified portfolio of metrics that need to be considered for multidimensional success.

How can increasing the metric of happiness contributed to your bottom-line?

Since 1971, the country of Bhutan decided to start measuring "gross national happiness" (GNH) instead of gross domestic product (GDP).[32] The country is making the statement that it doesn't matter how much money they make if their people aren't happy. The happiness of the people is what matters the most, and what you measure and track grows. That's the golden rule. When Bhutan started to measure happiness, it started to grow. There is no coincidence there. I believe that there is something to be said for measuring differently, for choosing a different mindset about measurement and what's important to measure.

The United States has one of the highest GDP's in the world, and it also has one of the highest unhappiness and unfulfillment rates. On the World Happiness Report, America's happiness dropped from number three in 2007 to number 19 in 2016.[33] The significance of the drop is shocking, though arguably not surprising when we look at our singular drive toward

[32] https://www.theguardian.com/world/2012/dec/01/bhutan-wealth-happiness-counts
[33] https://www.shape.com/lifestyle/mind-and-body/world-happiness-report-2017-shows-americans-unhappy
http://worldhappiness.report/ed/2017/

achievement. As a nation, we are stuck in the box of the one-dimensional leadership.

Why are we focusing on a limited metric instead of a whole metric model?

Changing our metrics and measurements has to be the way of the future, because a one-dimensional, bottom-line metric leaves a big wake of collateral damage in its path, especially when that dimension points solely to the bottom line. The wake of damage spills through the organization. It also perpetuates by giving future leaders and companies permission to measure success and be created in the same way. It creates a cycle of non-excellence, based on a metric that doesn't include what really matters. You want happiness, fulfillment, contribution, collaboration and impact, and what you want matters. We need to change the lens of what we perceive to be valuable and diversify our metric portfolio for sustainability and growth.

Fundamentally, this is about shifting the mindset about where value comes from. Time is not relative to value. Money is not value. It takes some irresponsibility to own a level of understanding of what value is. Because it's not time or money. The only thing that is equal to value is value.

The only thing that is equal to value is value.

Is what you currently value valuable?

Shift the focus from the bottom-line metric that you are placing either the majority or all of the value on. Diversify your metrics to cover all aspects of value: happiness, health, relationships, fulfillment, contribution, collaboration, impact, etc. The bottom line is only one piece of the equation. Diversify for sustainability and for growth. What happens to genetics the further you spread them apart? They get better. Diversify your metrics. Personal leadership involves the ability to take all the external systems and metrics and take responsibility for owning them internally, within ourselves. Happiness is the highest probability of impact to ourselves from ourselves.

What does it look like to create impact to yourself for yourself?

What does it look like to care deeply about yourself?

What if you as the founder are equally important in the process? Rather than sacrificing yourself, your happiness is part of the greater good. If you are willing to take on that mindset, that how you feel matters, it will be fuel for you, and not something to shy away from in the process. These are things that the leader in this new era of leadership gets to bake into their identity before they even get started on this endeavor, because *how you start is how you finish.*

The new era of leadership says we're not willing to sacrifice the founder anymore. Regardless of how much money a company makes, if the founder is not deeply fulfilled and happy, and connected to themselves, the company is considered unsuccessful. What if *the founder's happiness and fulfillment* was a metric? Game changer, right?

Great happiness and fulfillment are naturally occurring results of the expansion process itself. Sustained happiness is about marrying the happiness-evoking process and being happy for happiness' sake – coming to a place where realize that you are enough just as you are (i.e. you expand) and discovering the existence of happiness and fulfillment where you are. You play the game for the love of the game. At the same time, desire continues to build your internal fire. Happiness and fulfillment do not mean stagnation or settling into a new status quo. You've chosen to venture outside the box and into the impossible so that you can continue to expand. The more you seek, the more that continues to pour into and fill your cup.

Take what you know about what makes you happy, what makes you fulfilled, what makes you expand and apply it to be present with yourself. The people I know who have the greatest presence embody who they are and what they're doing. If you look at people who are on the other side of that, they are not really saturated in their identity and purpose, and they're quite frantic. Their presence is spotty at best.

On the other side of the expansion process is the whole, complete leader. However, knowledge alone will not lead you there. Knowledge is only *potential* power, because it is useless without action. To know yourself is not the complete solution. Just because it's written on the doors of Delphi does not make it the end. To know what an expanded leader is marks only the beginning of what can be. The answer to ending the isolation, depression and unfulfillment of one-dimensional leadership is to be your whole, fully expressed, best version self...and to be yourself, you must be able to take what you now know and *apply it*.

In phase 1 of the new expanded model of leadership, we talked about letting go of the idea of responsibility – making leadership about passion and the full expression of yourself. In phase 2, we covered identifying and living from the version of yourself that is whole and complete – making leadership a state of being and about the full realization of your potential. "Leadership is passion" is about discovering what you want, cultivating that passion and allowing yourself to be irresponsible. "Leadership is a State of Being" is about living out your limitless potential, owning your worthiness, being a gift and embodying the leader than you are. Being happy, fulfilled and commercially successful can only occur when you live in full expression of yourself and in full realization of your potential.

The 3 Aspects and 3 Motivators of Expanded Leadership

The 3 aspects of expanded leadership are:

1. Self,

2. Organization &

3. Impact

Let's begin with the self, before moving onto the organization and global impact. It starts with you, because an organization and culture cannot be anything that the leader is not. The organization is purely of a reflection of the best and worst parts of the leader. Since this is true, then it begs the investigation of an important point: if the two things employees desire the most are acknowledgment and growth, then shouldn't these also be the #1 priority for the founder to do for themselves at the highest level? Absolutely. Why? Firstly, because you deserve them as well. Secondly, because acknowledgement and growth are about transforming your knowing into action. Doing so allows you to operate from a standpoint of a much deeper understanding of how to bring these critical elements of human fulfillment forward to everyone else.

For far too long, leaders have "understood" that creating culture is good, yet they had zero embodiment of what great culture truly entails. Culture is not about bringing in bean bag chairs and catered lunches; it's about creating an environment that fosters growth and connection, with a unified vision toward creating a better tomorrow. On the flip side, this means that if you struggle with not feeling as though you are enough (you aren't acknowledged and growing), then it becomes difficult to create a cohesive culture. If you are disconnected from your worthiness, you will not only attract employees that are just the same, you will also be unable to grow into the desired culture and leadership structure...that is, until it everything gets transformed through the expansion process.

What are the elements of self that are crucial metrics of the expansion process for you as a leader? There are six key points of measurement:

- **Beliefs** – What beliefs do you have that are preventing you from expanding? Let go of those limiting beliefs.

- **Vision** – The visionary leaders reflects their inner game discipline in their outer game results. How powerful is your current vision (i.e. how much have your employees fallen in love with your vision)? How can you clarify, strengthen and communicate your vision to be the best it can be?

- **Passion** – What is your current level of impact? What is your ideal level of impact? What can you do to bridge the gap between the two?

- **Personal Patterns of Excellence** – What patterns contribute to you operating from a place of excellence? Open up the process of asking yourself about and observing the patterns that contribute to excellence in your leadership. There is no "one-size fits all" answer. Let go all previous suggestions and determine what works for you.

- **Prioritization of Connection to Self and Others** – Expansion can only happen when people are at the heart of everything you do. You as the leader are at the heart of your leadership – prioritize your connection to yourself, then extend that same care to others.

- **Expansion of Self-Actualization** – Take the necessary time to clarify your beliefs, your purpose and all that you stand for. Let it be your guidepost. Self-actualization is not optional.

By now, you should have a grasp on the inner-game discipline required to realize expansion; so let's talk about the outer-game systems required to bring it to the levels of the organization and global impact, and how to maintain it.

The self, organization and impact of expanded leadership are fueled by the 3 motivators of the new era of leadership:

1. Contribution

2. Collaboration &

3. Impact

Motivator #1: Contribution

The first motivator of the new era of expanded leadership is contribution – the action of giving from full expression of yourself and the full realization of your potential. Effective contribution can only happen from a full cup. Leading with this new contribution mindset shifts the old paradigm of productivity and achievement focus, to a new focus on depth of richness for everyone involved in what you are creating.

It's okay to put you first, and be irresponsible, to thereby be responsible and make a contribution – a dent in the universe. Fulfilling your potential only happens when you dive into yourself and give from a full cup. Realize that you are a gift – one that needs to growth through the constant nourishment of happiness and fulfillment. This is the revolution of self and the expanded picture of multidimensional leadership. When you embrace your worthiness and worth, then you embrace your full potential. The more worthy you feel that you are, the more you feel safe and are willing to risk. The more you are willing to risk, the bigger you are willing to dream.

The leader who feels acknowledged, and who is growing and confident, blends compassion into everything they do. Their legacy goes down in history as something that moved the world one step closer to utopia.

You only expand to the capacity in which you feel safe. The impossible becomes an ever-expanding idea that anyone can embrace as you expand as a person. You just have to want it and to realize your worth in building it, because when you do, the contribution made in the impossible ripples through the organization and beyond, creating an expanded universe.

What does this new model and metrics look like at the organizational and universal level? Turn the page.

From Competition to Collaboration

If it's possible to get people to do what you want out of fear, how infinite does innovative possibility become under the umbrella of love?

Is it at least possible to create the same level of output acting from love?

Is it possible to create more output?

Bypassing employee happiness and growth can no longer be acceptable.

A globally awesome company can only be created in one way.

Be awesome to the people in the organization.

Be awesome to the end user.

Ultimately, be awesome to yourself.

Challenge yourself to imagine what would be possible when acting from compassion.

It is possible to grow in numbers *and* grow in depth.

And that's a beautiful picture.

As an expanded leader, you create an organization that comes as a function of your wholeness, potential and full expression. By embracing yourself, your rawness, your authenticity and self-acceptance, you have a framework to design an environment and culture that fosters connection, appreciation and growth. Happiness within the organization is a function of the leader's happiness. If you, as the founder, show up aligned, worthy, clear, and overflowing with happiness, fulfillment and care for yourself, the trickle-down effect to the organization, end user and beyond can only be awesome. You need to focus on creating a culture that not only grows in numbers, but also grows in depth…and depth requires accountability for the whole of each and every individual.

The mainstream model tyrannical leader believes that treating people like shit is a necessary precursor to accomplishment and achievement. This mentality presumes that the lash is more powerful than the love…and yet, we have seen massive movements led from love. The stance is one of expanding consciousness and expanding the mindset that it is not only possible to create the same output, but that love may serve as an even better motivating tool.

Can you see your production increasing when you lead from love?

Happiness is the new metric by which we measure the impact of leading from love at the organizational level. Keep in mind part of your legacy is the quality of life you create for those who work with and for you. Do not bypass the employees in the name of the end user or the bottom line. Instead, know that focusing on happiness, compassion and collaboration is what will fuel your bottom line.

How does happiness directly connect to a better bottom line? When employees feel happy, they have more energy. When they have more energy, they are more creative, they are more engaged, and that leads to better production. In addition, if employees are happy, it probably means they feel safe. If they feel safe, then it likely means that they don't feel like they're working in a cut-throat environment, where the majority of time and energy would go into protecting themselves rather than taking risks for innovation and expansion. Those risks are needle-moving activities for business growth.

Think of the organization like an army or team. In ancient Greece, the Spartans were highly unified as a team. What allowed them to be one of the most powerful fighting forces in the world? Trust. New Zealand national rugby team, the All Blacks, are the most-winning team of all sports of all time and have been called "the greatest team in sports history."[34] That's staggering to think

---

[34] https://www.foxsports.com.au/rugby/rugby-world-cup-2015/wallabies-lost-because-the-all-blacks-are-the-greatest-sporting-team-in-the-history-of-world-

about: the most winning team of all time of all sports. One of the things they focus on most is being a unified team. Each member of the team feels a deep responsibility for moving the team forward and legacy forward. "Leave the jersey in a better place than when you found it." is their motto.

Building Compassionate Teams

What is an organization? It's a team. If every member of the team feels responsible for moving the vision forward, what you have is massive synergy. The greatest sports teams in the world understand the importance of a strong team. A team of "A players" who ball hog and fight amongst each other will never be better than a team of "B players" unified with clear eyes full hearts and a sense of team.

Imagine for a moment that your organization goes down in history as one of the greatest of all time. And the reason for this success is not only because of its commercial earning power – that is only the tip of the iceberg. It happens because you pour so much into your own personal development as a leader and care so much about creating an expanding and enriched culture that those who work for the organization have amazing lives.

sport/news-story/b9c9ee8798d80a9ef61023e502f1e332?sv=faf388a7cdfb7f9e7be225925f4562c0

Imagine you come into the office and it is thriving at a heart level. Trust connection productivity and innovation and a deep sense of care for the customer is the daily norm, and not the rare exception. When such synergy exists, your energy, as the founder, can go into leading, creating and pioneering, instead of managing, resenting and barking. You feel like what you have created really matters to each and everyone involved. This is not a pipe-dream my friend, this is the way of the future. This is what you have always wanted, and I am here to tell you that it is possible. The past does not equal the future. You can become a beacon of this new era.

The past does not equal the future.

You can become a beacon of this new era.

The elements of the organization that are crucial metrics in relation to happiness, deep culture and the resultant expanded products and services are:

- **Safety** – Do employees feel safe or do they feel like they are expendable?
- **Trust** – Can employees trust their leaders/superiors?
- **Kindness** – Is kindness a major focus from the top down?
- **Responsibility** – Do employees have a role where they feel deeply connected to moving the vision forward?

- **Feeling a part of something that matters** – Does the vision make them come alive?

As a leader, if you feel totally protected and provided for by yourself, then you're going to be willing to venture into the impossible and fail as many times as necessary, to get to your goal and make a contribution. When you extend this essence and embed it into the culture of the company, you give permission to the employees to do the same. You give them permission to trust, to connect, to grow and to expand. They feel safe – a stark contrast from a culture where employees are afraid and limited (as is the case with the tyrannical leader). When everyone feels like the work atmosphere is a place where they can take risks, then you all win. You set the example by demonstrating and promoting expansion. The net result of this is a cycle of synergy where everyone feels like they are protected and provided for knowing that someone has their back.

When it comes to an organization, a lot of the innovation comes from within. It's not the founder doing all the innovation. It comes from the team. But the team has to feel safe and open enough to expand. Steve Jobs could have never created the Apple legacy by himself. He needed other people who were also willing to be risky, to engineer and to think different. He needed to rally those who felt safe enough to risk and venture into the impossible...and from there came all of Apple's innovation and breakthroughs. It was okay to break things and fail along the way, knowing that was a necessary part of the dream and contribution.

If the people on your team are doing a great job, doing what they're supposed to be doing, the most responsible thing you can do is to allow them to do what they do. When things don't go how you'd like them to go, there are typically only a few reasons: either they were not clear about exactly what to do and how to do it, they don't have the skill set to do it or they aren't the right person for the job. Rapid expansion can lead to fast hiring at the detriment of the organization. When people are brought in to fill a role that are ultimately not a great fit for, this is the responsibility of the leader. It is your job to make sure that the right people are in all of the right places. When this happens, and you are able to step back and give the employees autonomy, it creates high levels of trust. It also allows the leader to free up bandwidth to focus on things that matter.

Remember that, as a leader, you are *not* a manager...and certainly not a micro-manager. Your job is to lead, and as a leader your number one role is to create leaders by giving people the space and freedom to do their jobs. Lead with compassion and give your people the capacity to innovate. Instead of living in fear, as they would with tyrannical leadership, they can live in the state of expansion and grace. The end result is more creative, happy and productive teams.

These metrics are more than how much money you can

make from the next product. Caring matters and caring about the people in your organization matters. If you're in the world of products, the "where," "how" and "who" that has created your product matters. A lot of people merit Apple's success on the fact that they're one of the top five businesses in the world from a numbers perspective. The old metric of thinking would suggest that they are a great company because they are financially successful. It creates the belief that leadership is great because of the bottom line. While there are obviously a lot of awesome things about Apple, we also know that at certain levels of leadership, there are things that were not so awesome.

When 150 Chinese workers are staging a suicide protest at Foxconn (manufacture of parts for Apple), there's a problem.[35] If an organization has installed suicide nets because they believe (or know) that, left to their own devices, employees would jump out of the fucking window or off the roof, what kind of team does that create? What type of legacy is that? We must no longer be willing to turn a blind eye to what happens to workers just because record breaking sales numbers and raving customers. Each and every life must matter.

The expanded leadership model means changing the metrics for measuring success to include the impact of happiness and fulfillment on the bottom line and for everyone in the

---

[35] https://www.telegraph.co.uk/news/worldnews/asia/china/9006988/Mass-suicide-protest-at-Apple-manufacturer-Foxconn-factory.html

organization. It means accounting for all dimensions of excellence.

How many leaders have taken the time to execute this to the level we're talking about here? In our world, we see examples of it. Gandhi's movement was done with love, creating a following of countless people. Many of the examples we have are not in a business context. The new era of expanded leadership means having a spillover of love-lead movements into the organizations.

When people are cohesive, synergistic and happy, magic can happen. What happens to music bands when band members are unified and happy? They go straight to the top. What happens when they start to fight with each other? They plummet, because there is discourse and chaos. That's how bands break up and you never hear from them again. Consider a family dynamic where everyone is happy and cohesive. Compare what that creates to what families who are not happy creates. How can happiness not impact the bottom line? In a very strategic way, happy employees are more productive, period. More production creates more output, more output means more ROI.

Creating Deep Culture

Do you truly understand what culture is? An organization doesn't necessarily have to have more people come into it for it to grow; it can grow in depth. The depth of the organizational will always be synonymous with the depth of the leader. If you bring a lot of dimension and depth to the organization, to the culture, then you create a culture where people feel safe enough to be able to have that depth as well. Your employees open themselves to being more fully expressed and in full realization of their potential.

Deep culture has to do with having an organization of multidimensional people. There is room for trust, creativity, innovation and risk-taking. Because of the atmosphere of compassion and collaboration, not only does one-dimensional, bottom-line agenda get handled, but it becomes transformed, because of the multidimensional depth that everyone is bringing to the table. In this organization, even when the conversation is about a single, one-dimensional topic, there are always multiple dimensions at play. You, as a whole and complete leader, are inviting others to bring their whole selves to the table. That's really what we're talking about. The conversation gets transformed from "how do we move the ball forward?" to "how do we play a completely different game?" There is room for expansion, and you are all doing it as a unified whole.

Motivator #2: Collaboration

The second motivator of expanded leadership is collaboration, which occurs when the expanded organization shifts from competition to collaboration. Where being cut-throat was once the mask that hid motives for personal and organization expansion, the fear of being backstabbed is replaced by connection. In the new era, being irresponsible does not mean creating a culture that is unrestrained, disrespectful and lacking collaboration.

Uber CEO, Travis Kalanick was asked to resign by shareholders in 2017 after months of questions about leadership. The Uber workplace culture was described as one of "sexual harassment and discrimination."[36] Kalanick drove forward a vision that went from 2009 start-up to a $70 billion business operating in 70 countries in 2017.[37] He went after the impossible and achieved some amazing things, however, the bedrock of what he created eroded, because there were pieces of the puzzle that were not resolved from the get go. Had he been willing to operate as the whole version of himself, lead with self-care, and compassion, and help his employees do the same, Uber may not have been left trying to regain its footing.

We have seen the opposite enough to understand that the possibilities of what happens when you have a culture of expanded leaders is beautiful. Ultimately, on a large scale, we create a mass culture of collaboration, where there was once competition. Individually, from a founder or leader standpoint, you'd have people who feel whole, feel complete. Happiness and fulfillment matter at both the individual and organizational level, as does

---

[36] https://www.nytimes.com/2017/06/21/technology/uber-ceo-travis-kalanick.html

[37] https://www.nytimes.com/2017/02/22/technology/uber-workplace-culture.html

expansion. Creating a company with universe denting power means being responsible for future generations as well. Allow what you build to inspire future and current leaders to do things differently in a way that creates even more growth and connection.

In order to successfully achieve such a vision, it will require other people to be involved to fuel and continue your legacy beyond your lifetime. You want employees to rally behind the unified vision and the consumer to feel like they are part of something much larger than a transaction. Many great dreams have died before they even saw the light of day, simply because the founder of that dream lacked the ability to paint a vivid picture that others can get behind. If you have a vision with an end result that makes the world a better place, then it deserves not only a chance to come to life, but the absolute *best* chance possible. Wouldn't you agree?

The quality of our lives is a function of the quality of our communication. The greatest leaders in history were able to communicate exactly what they saw in their mind. Know that you are worthy, be willing to risk and venture into the impossible, communicate your dream in vivid detail, excite your team and move forward together to make a dent in the universe.

Expanded Leadership is about the founder finding happiness and fulfillment through full self-expression and full realization of your potential, so that can be a catalyst for the people in the organization to do the same. It's all about people, with the big-picture objective of unifying to feel a part of something that matters – something that can create an impact which ultimately is about helping other people. Impact is about people not money. You can't measure impact by the amount of money that a company makes. You measure it by how many lives are improved by what you do. When people feel happy and fulfilled on a global scale, everything shifts.

Highest Probability of Deep Impact

How far does one's head have to turn until an eye becomes blind?

A dark world is a product of a life lived entirely in the mind.

Is it not the hearts of those we seek to empower that we long so desperately to liberate?

We seem to get further away from our humanity regardless of how much technology may iterate.

The peak of the human experience is not love, nay love is the foundation.

Say we get to mars without compassion, would we not be haunted by the same frustration?

Trust me when I say life is better together.

Yesterday today and forever.

We live in an era of hacking and shortcuts, and it has gotten us away from understanding that the excellence ends up getting hacked out of the process too. In reality, to create something truly world-changing, excellence is necessary. There is no hack or shortcut. Wanting to create deep organizational cultures and happiness for yourself and the organization is a different mindset. It's a different approach to how things get created. Having an approach that is beyond a bottom-line, one-dimensional measurement defines how powerful your vision and impact become. The new era metrics must include impact.

How does the impact of continuous releases of marginally better products differ from a product that was built from love? Would the end users experience be improved when a leader leads from wholeness and overflow, rather than emptiness and sacrifice?

Client Story

Samantha Skelly isn't looking to quickly scale into a multi-million-dollar company. As the founder of Hungry for Happiness, she envisions a world in which women no longer feel compelled to diet – in which they have a strong connection to their body and its intuitive powers. Revolutionary of the weight-loss industry, her organization examines the individual and underlying causes of eating disorders. She believes in changing people's lives, changing the conversation around food and body, and getting people to stop being addicted to suffering, in order to be able to step into the world and thrive. Their goal? To help one million women end dieting by 2020.

Never afraid to hustle, Samantha was a "go-go-go" type of

founder from the start...though what she was creating was happening at the cost of her mental health. As a people-pleaser who cares deeply, it was easy to get caught up in the busyness of the organization. Flooded by her own emotionality when she doesn't give herself time and space to reset, she can become resentful and everything becomes tainted. When she sacrifices herself, she approaches her team and clients differently – out of alignment with how she wants to.

When you aren't giving from a full cup, it's easy to feel that your employees or end users are taking from you. In truth, they can only take what is available. Resent happens when you don't have anything to give and give it anyway. In our work together, we learned that it was important for Samantha to be able to disconnect and gain perspective, in order to provide deep impact to the end user. When she took time for meditation and retreats, it fueled back into her company and to the end user. By filling her cup first, Samantha discovered that giving from overflow not only changed her end users experience of her organization, it changed her experience of them.

Hungry for Happiness is rapidly on its way to becoming a billion-dollar company, while disrupting the diet industry and working with thousands of women across the globe. Samantha focuses on aligning her energy with the right people she wants to attract. That is what is *real* for her – it's what fuels her business to have the highest probability of deep impact. Over the years of running her organization, she discovered that the more tactical things, such as marketing funnels or endlessly tweaking copy to reach the right audience, often didn't work for her. Her drive wasn't to rapidly expand the bottom line; her drive was to expand the people she helps.

Deep impact requires an expanded mindset. Samantha credits her growth to her team, and their commitment to the mission. Building something from the heart, she created an environment where her people felt free to thrive – not in terms of hierarchy, but in the sense of "we are all in this together." The mission isn't about her; it's about changing the conversation around food and body as a whole.

The secret to her global impact is, in her words, "The ability to have the right people in the right seats, with all the arrows pointing in the right direction...and it all comes down to 'energetics.' The right skills don't always align. People have to care about the mission and be heart-centered." Her organization's values include:

- **Personal accountability**

- **Being mission-driven** – doing the work for the mission

- **Intimacy & connection** (too often lost in the automation of online business) – maintaining it within the culture as they scale

- **Authenticity & integrity** – in her words: "clean as fuck" on the inside. What you see on the outside is what's going on inside.

What is the result for the end user? Samantha and Hungry for Happiness pride themselves on knowing exactly what their ideal client wants, and they aren't afraid to destroy things that don't work, in order to create what is better. Her motto? "Be attached to the most ultimate outcome you can create, thereby detaching yourself from current systems." The deeper seed that permeates her mindset is the fact that they will only be successful and have a business if they are more concerned about the transformation of their end users than the money in the bank.

Focusing on deep impact means not always taking the easy way; though as Samantha can attest, when the founder and organization are most concerned with the happiness of clients, "That's how we're going to win in the long term."

Hungry for Happiness is being built to outlive Samantha, and she is willing to see the bottom line go down a bit to make adjustments, in order to create a legacy and an unshakeable user experience. To her, this is a movement rather than a business or brand. She wants end users to feel like their programs are the best thing they've ever done. Why? Because she sees the highest version of others and only cares about helping people realize that.

The expanded leader is one who helps all others

expand...or as Samantha puts it, "You align with people who have the same values and you dance."

On a bigger scale, the likely end results of expanded leadership with a focus on the metrics of happiness, fulfillment and contribution are even better products and services, because your employees have way more bandwidth for creativity and imagination – the things that fuel bigger and better ideas. The potentiality of outcome is measured in quantum leaps in the quality, capacity and ability of products and services that hit the marketplace.

Motivator #3: Impact

In this new expanded model, ROI remains important. The difference is that it stands for something very different. ROI in the new context stands for *Ripple of Impact*. For far too long, business success has been measured simply by the bottom line, by money. While there is nothing wrong with this, is it incomplete and does not take into account the multidimensional pieces that a expanded movement or organization requires. Ripple of Impact focuses on all of the areas that matter most. In other words:

- the human lives that are impacted *by* the organization *and*

- the human lives that are impacted *within* the organization.

The elements of impact that are crucial metrics in relation having the positive effects of expansion spill over to end users, investors and the globe include:

- **Deep love and respect for the end user.**

- **A dedication to deep impact for the investor.**

- **Innovation of self and organization**, due to a commitment to constant and never-ending improvement (kaizen).

- **Understanding of legacy** – creating something that will not only outlive the founder, but also improve with time.

Up until now, it has somehow been permissible for major commercial success to happen off the back of glorified slave labor. Moving forward, this must no longer be tolerable. In order to create the utopian world that you and I care so much about, it must not only be intolerable, we must bring forth the exact opposite. As a leader, you must come to the conclusion that the impact that your organization makes on the lives of those who are a part of it is just as important as anything else. Future leaders should want to model how you create culture in excellence within the organization rather than just modeling how you created excellence commercial success on the heals of non-excellent means. You cannot make the world a better place, when those who are helping to do so are miserable.

Do we not have a responsibility to everyone involved, to bring more happiness richness and expansion to their lives?

I believe that this idea should not be the peak of leadership. Given the current landscape of leadership, this may sound like a worthy ideal; however, what this ideal should be is the most basic and fundamental principle of how you create anything that involves other people. We must expand our mindset and believe that it is possible to dent universe without creating a wake of collateral damage along the way. Isn't it ironic that some of the most visionary leaders – people who want to do the impossible – buy into archaic beliefs that the only way to do so is through massive sacrifice for themselves and those who are part of the vision?

Is it any wonder why the majority of businesses fail?

Long-term, a driver cannot continue win the Grand Prix while sacrificing the tires on the car and oil in the engine. Can they still be expected to win? Yes. Is it possible? Sure. Doesn't make any sense? Not at all. The over-arching model for how to be successful cannot be by giving up the majority of things that matter in life. Quality matters. Impact matters. If you do not believe that there is a more holistic way to create success, then that path can never exist, and the past is destined to repeat itself.

Deep Impact for End Users

Every time Apple releases a new iPhone, they sell out. At the Apple stores, there's a line down the street, and the iPhone is sold out. Once the cart opens online, it's literally moments before they sell out. Pretty impressive. What's not impressive is the lack of change from one model to the next. There's not much difference between models from the last five or six years. The camera is marginally better. The operating system is essentially the same. The phone has all the same features, it does the same thing as the model before it. Even the upgrades are only marginally better.

A seller's world is only as excellent as the consumer requires it to be.

Having a deep impact on the end user extends far beyond offering as little improvement to the end user unit and experience as possible. A model that settles for only marginally better products negates looking at how to make things exponentially better. Why is this happening? Why have we made this an acceptable culture? Like many organizations, Apple doesn't have to offer more than marginal product upgrades, because the consumer is okay with the current level of product progress. A seller's world is only as excellent as the consumer requires it to be. If the next iPhone came out and the majority of end users were more vocal in the phone not being much different and announced that they would no longer buy the phone until Apple was willing to give a truly deep impact with every product update, what would Apple then have to do?

Are you currently operating with the objective of deep impact?

You don't wait until the consumer requires deep impact of you. Come to the table requiring it *yourself*. There is a huge difference between being asked to do something (doing it reactively, out of necessity) and choosing to take responsibility yourself (proactively, before even being asked). Expanded, multidimensional leadership is about operating at a different level, because you are making the choice up front to have deep impact. You are starting with the end in mind, and the end is creating the most excellent experience possible. You do this from the onset, because that's what *you* want for the people – your employees, your end users and your investors.

Deep impact requires quantum leaps: creating and innovating at a level that's beyond anything that you've done so far. Marginal increases that don't require people to go beyond the known in order to achieve them. They don't challenge you as the leader to venture into the impossible. Deep impact requires the incorporation of both irresponsibility and impossibility. It creates a win-win-win, leading to happiness and fulfillment for you, the organization and the end user. Creating products with exponential excellence has great reward. As much as Apple may release moderately better versions with each iPhone model, those versions are still leaps and bounds above what most of the marketplace is offering. If they can have such massive success getting away with how they currently play the game, what would happen if they totally shifted and chose to play at an expanded level?

All of the happiness, fulfillment and impact-based metrics we're talking about in the organization and in the end user experience must be reflections of the founder themselves. It's an interesting mirror. If the bottom line is releasing marginally better versions of a product and expecting people to pay full price or more for them is okay, that points at a certain level of care for the customer. If the customer is a mirror of the founder, then that points to a level of value the founder has for themselves.

Playing the game with the objective of having deep excellence-driven impact can only mean more success. If you put your foot on the gas even more, you are going to go faster. If all of the elements of the vehicle are built with excellence, then you are going to go the distance, creating happiness, fulfillment and impact for yourself, your employees, the end users and investors.

Deep Impact for Investors

If you want to create a business with a layer of leadership

that is unlike anything that's ever been created, but you have investors who are bought into the old way of doing things, it's a train wreck from the start. Even your investors must buy into a model of operating from a place of being whole, complete and collaborative. Investors must make the quantum leap and have the mindset of this new era of success and leadership. They need to realize that not only do they need to measure the bottom line as a metric of success, but also measure the highest probability of deep impact for the end user and the happiness and excellence of the organization. They realize that *all* of these things matter.

This is a very new breed of investor. The shift of the new era of expanded leadership is not only changing the mindset of you as the leader, it is transforming the focus of the employees, end users and investors – everyone across the board. There is an understanding in expanding things like happiness, fulfillment and wholeness of the individual – things that are not directly related to the bottom line – because those with the expanded mindset understand that these things *do* impact the bottom line. Just because these metrics have not been grown, attended to or measured in the past, doesn't mean they're not directly related to the bottom line.

There is no such thing as a company; what we're always talking about is people. That's all an organization, end users or investors are: people. That's all that business is; it's people. Knowing that everything you are building is about people (yourself included), it then becomes clear that investing in and growing people is the primary ingredient of growing the bottom line of your business. When you look at it this way, it is pretty obvious.

Let's paint a picture: you have a world where investors are multidimensional in wanting to help you create a deep impact for your employees and end users. They understand as well as you that what is being created has much more depth than what is currently being measured for the bottom line. With the desire to impact happiness and fulfillment for everyone involved – from vision to execution to end product – they're on board and championing you to make this dream a reality. These expanded investors are ultimately investing in a better world.

As a founder, you understand the importance of helping yourself, your employees and your end users be fully expressed and in helping them realize their full potential. You are willing to be an example of that, and bring this essence through the organization, from the top down. What type of organization would that create? What type of legacy would that create for other generations to be able to model for their businesses? Pretty astounding I think.

An Expanded World

Dystopian shit show or utopian wonderland?

The world is racing towards a tipping point.

You can feel it.

It's so clear, the sound of our destiny.

Unmistakable, it echoes beyond my ears through the rest of me.

It's not the day or this life I'm trying to seize, it's simply the moment.

I'm falling in love with the now.

It mutually feels like my proponent.

I sometimes feel like I've arrived too late.

The scales are tipping.

The stars with their candor artfully designed my meander to attend my fate.

Is it too late?

It's been said there are two impossible words always, and never.

But I'll never stop always dancing with forever.

The world is rapidly approaching a tipping point of utopia or dystopia. With current methods and models, we are tipping the scales in the least favorable direction: dystopia. We've all seen the sci-fi movies that depict the future as a place that is dark, cold and environmentally degraded. The rich and powerful live in the clouds, while everyone else is left to toil away below. Virtual and augmented reality consume people's lives, they live out their fantasies and fall deeper into despair knowing deep down these are nothing but sexy forms distraction. For the elite, enough is never enough and greed fuels their desire for even higher profits, regardless of the cost and ramifications on the end user. Compassion and kindness are all-but-absent from day-to-day life.

Currently, slavery is at an all-time high[38]; deforestation is costing us 18.7 million acres of forests annually[39]; poverty, disease and malnutrition plague millions of people; and the ocean has a "garbage patch" the size of Texas in it[40]. Teen suicide is up 70% in

---

[38] https://www.reuters.com/article/us-britain-slavery-index/nearly-30-million-people-in-slavery-index-idUSBRE99F1A320131016
[39] https://www.worldwildlife.org/threats/deforestation
[40] https://www.nationalgeographic.org/encyclopedia/great-pacific-garbage-patch/

ten years[41], employee unhappiness sits at about 87% globally[42] and only 32% of North American employees are engaged[43]. Despite all of these horrifying facts, YOU only need to ask yourself one question: Is what you are creating in the world contributing to utopia or dystopia?

The big-picture of leadership is one of our rapidly approaching a crossroads. One road will take us to a dystopian society, where everything is dark, everyone is disconnected and technology is the peak of civilization. The other road is to utopia, where the peak of civilization is humanity, and there is connection and lightness. At this point, we can go either way. The reason I exist is to help the tip go toward the utopian path.

As leaders, it is not enough to drive profits and "go further faster," if it lands us with a miserable planet full of miserable people. At this moment in history, you are faced with a very real choice: you can either be part of the solution or part of the problem.

Having read this book, you now have a clear picture of what it means to be an expanded leader and what type of organization gets created when you understand the principles of helping yourself.

---

[41] https://www.usatoday.com/story/news/politics/2018/03/19/teen-suicide-soaring-do-spotty-mental-health-and-addiction-treatment-share-blame/428148002/

[42] https://www.forbes.com/sites/susanadams/2013/10/10/unhappy-employees-outnumber-happy-ones-by-two-to-one-worldwide/#58d11204362a

[43] http://news.gallup.com/businessjournal/188033/worldwide-employee-engagement-crisis.aspx

What is the ultimate point of expansion when we choose to operate from this multidimensional model? When you reach beyond the organization and live in alignment with the ideal trajectory, where does it lead? How does this feel?

In the beginning of the book, we talked about how it feels to be in the depths of despair, trapped in the confines of a one-dimensional model of leadership, unable to expand or fuel a culture that longs to grow. It was easy for you to imagine what it felt like to experience the pain and frustration of limited leadership, because that was most likely is where you were. I say where you *were,* because my hope is, by now, you've made a decision about the type of leader that you want to be.

The old model has left us unfulfilled and stifled on a global level. The opposite is a place of being fully expressed and living true to our full potential. By accepting expanded leadership, you're voting yourself into a group of people who have been called to create the utopian world that we all desire. As an expanded leader, you can imagine how your life, your organization and ultimately your impact will drastically change. From a life-perspective, you'll experience levels of fulfillment, and expression of yourself and your potential that you've never had before. As you read this, sink into the feeling of how outstanding that's going to be, and what that's going to mean for you individually. When you see other leaders experiencing the same, how does that change things on a global level?

In the expanded model, not only is your experience of life going to be radically enhanced, so will the experience of your family, your friends, but also your organization. Instead of knowing that you have employees by and large that are experiencing angst, stress and limitation, you can rest your head peacefully at night knowing that everyone in your organization is experiencing their own expansion and their own full expression through the universal dent that you're creating. You have a very clear understanding that collaboration will always outperform competition. Anyone who you might have previously seen as a competitor or threat becomes a collaborator who you can sit down on the same side of the table with. Ultimately, we're all in this for the same reason: to create an expanded world.

Ultimately, we're all in this for the same reason: to create an expanded world.

Instead of business being synonymous with a cutthroat environment where people are constantly trying to outdo and one-up each other, it can be something where ideas are shared. By adopting this new era model, we're redirecting the focus and intention on what it is to do business. Competition can only exist if there's greed and selfishness; as soon as we transcend that, then we understand that it's best when everybody wins…when everyone expands.

When bandwidth doesn't need to be used for scarcity and fear and protectionism, there is a synergistic effect that happens, and an entirely new layer of creativity and innovation gets to be experienced by everyone involved. The objective of the expanded world must be to create a collaborative perspective, where the intention is for everybody to win, and there is freedom for everyone to share our ideas. If you meet someone and they give you a dollar, and you give them a dollar, then you both walk away with a dollar; but if you meet, and they share an idea with you and you share an idea with then, then you both walk away with two ideas. Creative and innovation are the fuel of global expansion.

Leaders Create Leaders

The compound effect of that expansion is quantum, simply because, the more you feed something that has a multidimensional return on investment, the more powerful it becomes. So, over time, this creates solutions, products and services that are far beyond what we would have imagined in the first place...and most definitely beyond anything created in the old one-dimensional model. By leading yourself to personal expansion, you are also paving the way for the people within the organization and your end users to expand.

We're not just talking about this anymore, we're living it.

We're creating an environment for limitlessness to exist. Limitlessness cannot exist in a box, created from scarcity and fear...it can only happen with creativity, innovation, imagination and collaboration. In the utopian world, one of the key drivers, or motivators, is expansion – it has to do with the constant and never-ending expansion of one's own potential. In a dystopian society, what happens is the opposite, where most people's potential is limited because of the way that society works.

Creating a new model for leadership is not something we can do; it is something we must do.

In the ideal utopian society, leaders are expanding to a larger degree and the corporations become stewards of the people, so that the people can experience just as much expansion. At the most global level, embracing the new expanded model of leadership equals a world where there are significant increases in the quality of people's lives, and everything in between. You would see a drastic improvement in happiness, fulfillment and wealth around the world. It's about allowing everyone to thrive...rather than have these class systems where some people are at the top and most people are at the bottom and have nothing. The expanded world model allows far more people to experience financial abundance, realize every type of expansion and fulfill every type of abundance.

This is an opportunity for anyone who feels called to step

into that expanded role. It gives the same opportunity to every area of the world that currently has major challenges like a lack of water, health or energy. It gives all of those areas and people the absolute highest probability of finding the most excellent solution.

The Highest Probability of the Most Excellent Solution

In the expanded model, the people of the world all have a chance to live the best life that they can have, and the world itself has the best chance of experiencing its natural state, rather than being destroyed and ultimately destroyed to a point of such deterioration that there's nothing we could do.

In the old model, our mindset so easily slipped into believing that what we have created is the best that things can be...or how they have to be. Remember that your greatest achievements can never be behind you. There is no possible way that this current state of leadership, organizations and the world, whatever they are, is the best that it can get.

Let me ask you again: what is the peak of human potential? No one knows, and we may never know. What we *do* know is that what we know right now, no matter how advanced we think we are, is but a speckle of what is possible. When we question the full picture of how we feel on a personal, organizational and global level, we can all agree that our potential is far beyond what we're experiencing at this moment.

This is our journey to see just how far we can go, in an expanded way. Many great leaders have wanted to go further faster, which is good, but it leaves out some of the fundamental important pieces of the puzzle. Right? If we go further faster, but we're still globally unhappy, how far have we gone? If we're going further faster without focus on individual expansion in the form of full expression and full realization of our potential, what we're really doing is going nowhere fast.

The truth is that there is no "there"; the journey is the destination. That sounds so cliché, but it is true. If we end up wherever we are going and we get there faster, arriving from non-excellence and sacrifice, then what's the point?

Leadership without sacrifice is about quality of expansion at the multiple dimensions of our whole selves, the whole of the organization and the entirety of humanity. It about quality of experience in the now. This is the Montessori of leadership, pushing us to create a new model that supports the expansion of the individual, in order to fuel the organization and global society with passion, creativity and innovation. It is our opening to reach to discover the peak of human potential at each and every turn – within ourselves, the organization and our highest probability of deep impact.

And so, the choice is yours: tips the scales toward utopia or let them slide into a dystopian shit show.

I know which way I'm pushing the needle. Are you with me?

Tip the scales toward utopia and expand your leadership.

Contact Shannon Graham for coaching,

workshops and speaking through

www.shannongraham.com

Made in the USA
San Bernardino, CA
12 July 2020

74675743R00140